学做中国菜
Learn to Cook Chinese Dishes
水产类 Seafood

外 文 出 版 社
FOREIGN LANGUAGES PRESS

前　言

朱熙钧

　　倘若不是想成为专业厨师，只是为了自家享用和飨客而学做中国菜，是无须拜师学艺的。中国主妇的厨艺几乎都是从她们的老祖母和母亲那里耳濡目染学来的；待到为人妻母之后，她们之中的一些有心人再借助菜谱加以揣摩，或与友邻切磋交流，制作出的菜馔有时竟然不逊于名店名厨的。当然，在中国的家庭中，擅长烹饪的男子也不在少数，而且饭店、餐馆中的名厨以男性居多。

　　这套《学做中国菜》丛书的编撰者都是烹饪大师，为了使初学者易于入门，他们以简明的文字介绍了每菜式的用料、刀法、制作步骤等。读者只须按照所列一一去做，无须多日便会熟能生巧，举一反三，厨艺大进。

　　《学做中国菜》系列丛书共九册，包括水产类、肉菜类、菜蔬类、豆品类、汤菜类、冷菜类、面点类、禽蛋类和家宴类。本册为《学做中国菜》系列丛书之一，汇集了烹调水产类的菜肴四十种。

　　水产类包括鱼、虾、蟹、贝类等。鱼虾、蟹又有淡水产和海水产之分。

　　水产类的烹饪因物料而异，一般对海鲜、鱼形不大的，以及虾类都应取其鲜嫩，烹饪就要用急火清蒸，或油温溜、炒。如清蒸鱼、炒虾仁、溜虾仁即是。鱼形较大，取其头或尾，或整条制作的，尤需要烹制时间较长。如红烧鱼等需要稍长的烧煮时间。

　　至于虾类，除带壳烹饪以外，更有出壳而成虾仁，然后挂蛋清、淀粉，用油温以快速清炒。而取其鲜嫩。否则，越烧越老。

　　水产类都有腥味，因而调料中必须有去腥味的酒、葱、姜之类。

　　对于骨刺较细而多的鱼，可以制成汤菜，使其鲜味入汤，且易出骨剔刺；鱼形小的可炸煮，使骨刺松脆酥软可食，无须出骨。对于肉质厚实的鱼，可切块、切条、切丝、切排、切末，甚至作成鱼卷、鱼茸而烹成菜肴。这样也有利于原汁入味。

　　鱼类在烹调之前要宰杀、刮鳞、斩鳍、挖腮，然后从胸部或背脊开膛，取出内脏，除出腹壁的黑膜。如果是用作鱼丝、鱼条、鱼卷这类菜式的还须剔除骨、刺，其方法是先切下鱼头，然后用刀从颈部紧贴鱼背骨横切至鱼尾，在尾部斩断鱼骨。半片鱼肉即随之脱落，再用刀沿肋骨的侧线割下鱼肋骨。另半片鱼肉也用同样的方法取下。虾类在烹制之前也应剪去须脚，抽出背筋，剔去泥肠。

Foreword

Zhu Xijun

You don't have to go to school to learn the art of Chinese cooking from a professional teacher if you just want to know how to cook for your own family or to entertain friends. In fact, almost without exception, Chinese women learn the skill by watching and working together with their mothers or grandmothers.

By the time they have become wives or mothers themselves, the most diligent ones will try to improve their techniques by consulting cook books and exchanging experiences with their neighbors and friends. In this way they eventually become as skilled as the best chefs in the established restaurants. It should be noted, of course, that most of the well-known chefs in famous restaurants are men, because many men in Chinese homes are just as good at cooking as their wives.

This set of Learn to Cook Chinese Dishes has been compiled by master chefs. They have used simple explanations to introduce the ingredients, ways of cutting, and cooking procedures for each Chinese dish. Readers can follow the directions and before long they are sure to become skilled in the art of Chinese cooking. The total set consists of ten volumes, covering freshwater and seafood dishes, meat dishes, vegetable dishes, courses made from soy beans, soups, cold dishes, pastries, dishes of eggs and poultry meat, food carving techniques and family banquet dishes. This particular volume presents more than forty dishes all made of aquatic products.

The major aquatic products in the book include fish, shrimp, crabs and shelled fish, and the first three categories include both freshwater ones and those from the sea.

The ways of cooking aquatic foods vary according to the size of the ingredients. If the sea item is small, as in the case of shrimps, maintaining tenderness should be the top priority. Consequently, quickly stir-frying with different sauces or steaming techniques should be adopted. Typical examples are steamed fish, stir-fried shrimps and quick-fried shrimps with distilled grains sauce. In the case of a large fish,

either part of it such as the head or the tail or the whole fish can be cooked in short time. Braised fish in soy sauce is one example.

Shrimps can be cooked in different ways with the shells on. Or the shells can be taken off and the shrimps are wrapped with egg white and/or cornstarch to stir-fry in lukewarm oil. This way their fresh tenderness can be preserved. Otherwise the longer they are cooked, the tougher they become.

All aquatic products carry a fishy smell. To remove this, cooking wine, scallions, ginger and similar fish-smell removing ingredients are essential.

Bony and fine-meat fish can be used to make soup so that, after cooking, it will be easier to remove the bones. Small-sized fish can be deep-fried so that the bones become crispy and edible.

Large fish that have thick meat can be cut into different sized chunks, slices, shreds, cubes, etc. Or they can be made into fish fluffing as an ingredient. Such methods of cooking allow the meat to fully absorb the contributing ingredients.

Before they are cooked, fish must be killed, the scales removed, the fins cut off, and the gills taken out. The fish must also be opened with a cut along its belly or on its back in order to clear out the inside parts, including the dark membrane inside the belly. To use the fish to make shreds or long and thin slices, the bones must also be removed. To do this, first cut off the head, and then hold the knife flat to cut one side of the fish from the bone, starting from the neck and going down to the tail. Half of the fish meat is thus obtained. Now use a chopper to cut sideways along the ribs to take out all the rib bones. Do the same to the other side of the fish. In cooking shrimps, their legs should be cut off, the back tendon pulled out and the intestine removed.

目 录
Contents

名词解释 Terms Used in Chinese Cooking

上浆：猪肉丝、猪肉片、牛肉丝、牛肉片、羊肉丝、羊肉片、鸡肉片在烹制前都要上浆。上浆大多用于滑溜、滑炒、清炒、酱爆等烹调方法。上浆好坏，直接影响烹调出菜肴的质量。上浆就是把切好的肉，用水冲洗净，放入盐、料酒、淀粉(有时也放鸡蛋)，拌匀后，向一个方向搅拌，感到有劲为止。

Coating (*shangjiang*): Shreds and slices of pork, beef, mutton and chicken have to be coated before they are cooked in such ways as slippery-frying, quick-frying and stir-frying. And how the meat is coated has a direct bearing on the quality of the cooked dish. The coating process involves first washing the cut meat, then adding in salt, cooking wine, and cornstarch(sometimes eggs are also used) and stirring well in the same direction until you feel it is a bit sticky.

刀工 Cutting techniques:

直刀法：就是指刀同砧板垂直的刀法，分切、剁、砍，切是一般用于无骨的主料,剁是将无骨的主料制成茸的一种刀法，砍通常用于加工带骨的或硬的主料。

Straight-cutting: Holding the knife perpendicularly over the chopping board to cut, chop and heavy-cut the main ingredient. Cutting is applied to boneless meat ingredients, chopping is done to turn boneless ingredients into pulp or paste and heavy-cutting is used when preparing meat with bones or other hard ingredients.

平刀法：是刀面与砧板平行的一种刀法，分推刀、拉刀。推刀就是把刀从刀尖一直推到刀根，拉刀就是把刀从刀根拉到刀尖。平切就是把刀一切到底。

Horizontal-cutting: Holding the knife flat against the chopping board to push it or pull it through the ingredients.Pushing means to push the knife through the ingredients from the knife's tip through to its end while pulling involves going through the ingredients from the end to the tip of the knife.

斜刀法：刀面同砧板面成小于90度夹角的刀法。

Slashing: To cut by holding the knife in an angle smaller than 90 degrees from the surface of the chopping board.

花刀：是在主料表面用横、竖两种刀法的不同变化，切(不断)出花纹，经加热后，主料卷曲成各种形状的刀法，有菊花形花刀，麦穗刀，鳞毛形花刀等。

Mixed cutting: To cut straight and then cross with sideways cuts to produce varied patterns. When heated, the ingredients cut in this way will roll up into different forms such as chrysanthemums, wheat ears and scales, according to the ways they are cut.

片：用切或片的方法将原料加工成薄片。质地硬的原料用切，质地软的用片的方法加工成薄片。

Slicing (*pian*):By either cutting or slicing to turn the ingredients into thin slices. Hard ingredients require cutting while soft ingredients require slicing.

丝：丝有粗细之分，一般在0.2-0.4厘米左右。一般先将主料切成0.2-0.4厘米的薄片，再将这些薄片排成瓦楞状，排叠要整齐，左手按稳主料，不可滑动，用刀把主料切成丝。

1

Shredding (*si*): The thickness of shreds usually varies between 0.2 (0±08 in) and 0.4 cm (0±16 in). First, either chunks of meat or vegetables are cut into thin slices of 0.2 to 0.4 cm in thickness. The slices are then arranged neatly like roof tiles.Pressed steadily underneath the left hand of the chef, the slices are finally cut into shreds.

条：条的成形方法，是先把主料切成厚片，再将片切成条，条的粗细取决于片的厚薄。

Strapping (*tiao*):Main raw materials are cut into thick slices that are cut again into straps the size of which is decided by the thickness of the slices.

粒：粒比丁小些一般在0.3厘米见方，切的方法同丁相同。

Grain-sized dicing (*li*): Cut in the same way as diced pieces, they are simply much smaller in size. The most common size is 0.3 cm (0.12 in) each side.

丁：先将主料切成厚片，再将厚片切成条，然后再切成丁。丁有大小之分，大丁在2厘米见方，小丁在1厘米见方。

Dicing (*ding*): Main raw materials are cut into thick slices that are cut into straps. In turn, the straps are reduced to diced pieces that may be as large as 2 cm (0.8in) on each side or as small as 1 cm (0.39 in) on each side.

末：末比粒还小，将丁或粒剁碎就可以了。

Mincing (*mo*): Ground ingredients are even smaller than grain-sized dices.Usually the diced pieces are chopped into mince.

茸：用排剁的方法把主料剁得比末还细。

Chopping to make a pulp (*rong*): To chop the materials, knife cut after knife cut into pieces even finer than minced materials.

块：块是采用切、砍、剁等刀法加工而成的。块分菱形块、方块、长方块、滚刀块等。

Cutting into chunks (*kuai*): Chunks are the result of perpendicular and sideways cutting as well as chopping. The chunks come in many shapes such as diamonds, squares and rectangles.

炸：是旺火加热，以食油为传热介质烹调方法，特点是火旺用油量多。

Deep-frying (*zha*): Heat the cooking oil over a hot fire and deep-fry the materials. This process is characterized by a hot fire and a large amount of oil.

炒：炒是将加工成丁、丝、条、球等小型主料投入油锅中，在旺火上急速翻炒成熟的一种烹调方法。炒分滑炒、熟炒、干炒等几种。滑炒是经过粗加工的小型主料先经上浆，再用少量油在旺火上急速翻炒，最后以湿淀粉勾芡的方法，叫滑炒。熟炒是把经过初步加工后的半成品，改切成片或块，不上浆，用旺火烧锅热油，放入半成品翻炒，再加佐料而成。煸炒和干炒是把主料煸一下，在热油锅急火炒至退水后，加佐料，起锅。

Stir-frying (*chao*): Put processed materials in the shape of diced pieces, shreds, straps, or balls into the heated oil and quickly stir them over a hot fire. There are several different ways of stir-frying. *Hua chao* (stir-frying with batter), for example, requires that the ingredients are put in a batter and then quickly stirred in a small quantity of oil over a hot fire.The final process is to apply the mixture of cornstarch and water. *Shu chao* (stir-frying precooked food) does not require that the materials be put into some kind of batter. Simply put the precooked materials into the wok and use a hot fire before adding spicing agents. *Bian chao* and *gan chao* (raw stir-frying) calls for the simmering of main ingredients, then quick-stir-frying over a hot fire until the juice is fully absorbed. Now add spicing agents and the dish is ready to serve.

溜：溜是先将主料用炸的方法加热成熟，然后把调制好的卤汁浇淋于主料上，或将主料投入卤汁中搅拌的一种烹调方法。

Slippery-frying(*liu*): First deep-fry the main ingredient and then top it with sauce or mix the main ingredient in the sauce.

爆：爆是将脆性主料投入适量的油锅中，用旺火高油温快速加热的一种烹调方法。

Quick-fry over high heat (*bao*): Put crispy materials into the wok with medium amount of oil and quickly stir the materials over high heat.

隔水炖：隔水加热使主料成熟的方法，叫做隔水炖。

Steaming in a container (*ge shui dun*): Put the main ingredient into a bowl or similar container and cook it in a steamer.

烧：烧是经过炸、煎、煸炒或水煮的主料，再用葱姜炝锅后，倒入翻炒，然后加适量汤水和调味品，用旺火烧开，中小火烧透入味 ，改用旺火使卤汁稠浓的一种烹调方法。

Stewing over medium,then high heat (*shao*): After putting scallions and ginger into the wok, put in the main materials that have been deep-fried, or stir-fried or boiled and stirred. Then add water and seasoning materials to cook over a hot fire until the ingredients boil. Turn the fire to medium or low to allow full absorption of the sauce into the ingredients before turning the fire hot again to thicken the sauce.

扒：扒是将经过初步熟处理的主料整齐地排放在锅内，加汤汁和调味品，用旺火烧开，小火烧透入味，出锅前，原汁勾芡的一种烹调方法。

Stewing and adding thickening (*pa*): Neatly arrange the main ingredient that has already been cooked,add water and flavoring materials and cook over a hot fire until it boils. Turn the fire to low to allow full absorption of the flavor. Thicken the sauce with the mixture of water and cornstarch before bringing the dish out of the wok to serve.

煮：煮是将主料放入多量的汤汁或水中，先用旺火煮沸，再用中小火烧熟的一种烹调方法。

Boiling (*zhu*): Put main materials of the dish into the wok with an adequate amount of water and cook it over a hot fire to the boiling point. Then continue to cook after turning the fire to low or medium.

烩：将加工成片、丝、条、丁等料的多种主料放在一起，炝锅翻炒后，用旺火制成半汤半菜的菜肴，这种烹调方法就是烩。

Precooking and then stewing (*hui*): First heat the oil in the wok, put in scallions and ginger and then put several kinds of main ingredients that have been cut into slices, shreds, chunks or dices to cook over a hot fire so as to create a dish of half soup and half vegetables and meat.

煎：煎是以少量油布遍锅底、用小火将主料煎熟使两面呈黄色的烹调方法。

Sauteing (*jian*): Put a small amount of oil into the wok and use a low fire to cook the main ingredient until it is golden brown on both sides.

蒸：蒸是以蒸汽的热力使经过调味的主料成熟或酥烂入味的烹调方法。

Steaming (*zheng*): Cook the materials that have already been prepared with flavoring agents by using hot steam.

拔丝：拔丝又叫拉丝，是将经过油炸的小型主料，挂上能拔出丝来的糖浆的一种烹调方法。

Crisp frying with syrup (*ba si*): Put small-size ingredients that have already been deep-fried into sugar syrup heated in the wok. When diners pick up the materials, long sugar threads are created.

焯水：就是把经过初加工的主料，放在水锅中加热至沸(主要为去腥味或异味)，原料出水后供烹调菜肴之用。焯水分冷水锅和热水锅。冷水锅就是主料与冷水同时下锅,水沸取出,适用于腥气重血量多的主料如牛肉、羊肉等。热水锅就是先将锅中水加热至沸，再将主料下锅，翻滚后再取出主料。适用于腥气小，血污少的主料如鸡、鸭、猪肉和蔬菜。

Quick boiling (*chao*): Put main ingredients into the pot and heat the water to boiling point(in order to remove fishy or other undesirable smells). Then cook the boiled ingredients. The quick-boiling process includes cold water boiling and hot water boiling. The former requires putting the ingredients into the pot toge ther with the cold water and then taking them out when the water boils. This process is often applied to such materials as beef and mutton,which contain a fishy smell and a lot of blood. The latter calls for heating the water in the pot to boiling point before putting the ingredients in.This is applicable to materials like chicken, duck, pork and vegetables that have a much weaker fishy smell and less blood.

油温表

油温类型	俗　　称	油温特点
温油锅	四成 70℃－100℃	无青烟，无响声，油面平静。
热油锅	五、六成热 110℃－170℃	微有青烟，油四周向内翻动。
旺油锅	七、八成热 180℃－220℃	有青烟，油面仍较平静，用勺搅动有响声。

Temperatures of cooking oil:

Category	Temperature	Features
Luke-warm	70ºC-100ºC 158ºF-212ºF	Smokeless, soundless, calm oil surface
Hot oil	110ºC-170ºC 230ºF-338ºF	Slight smoke, oil stirs from the side to the center of the wok
Very hot oil	180ºC-220ºC 356ºF-428ºF	Smokes, the surface remains calm and when stirred, sizzling sound is heard.

花椒：花椒是花椒树的果实，以籽小，壳厚紫色为好。味香麻，烹调肉类的调料。

Prickly ash (*hua jiao*): Seeds from prickly ash trees, which are small and light purple in color. They have a slight effect of numbness on the tongue. Used to cook dishes with meat.

椒盐：味香麻，是炸菜蘸食的调味品。把花椒和盐按1:3的比例在锅中，微火炒成焦黄，磨成细末，即成。

Pepper salt (*jiao yan*): This mixture is made by stirring one portion of peppercorns and three portions of salt in the wok until they turn crispy yellowish in color and release their fragrance. Then finely grind the mixture into powder. It serves as a seasoning for deep-fried dishes.

味精： 根据个人口味，也可不放味精，而使用适量的鸡精。

Monosodium glutamate and chicken bouillon: Though MSG is essential in traditional Chinese cooking, for many who do not find it agreeable, chicken bouillon can be used instead.

茴香： 小茴香是茴香菜的籽，呈灰色，似稻粒，有浓郁的香味。

Fennel seeds (*hui xiang*): Seeds of fennel plants, grey in color and similar to unhusked rice grains in shape, have a hot flavor.

大茴香： 又名八角、大料、形如星状，味甜浓，烹调肉类的调料。

Star anise (*da hui xiang*): In the shape of stars, they have a strong and sweet flavor. Mostly used in cooking meat dishes.

糟： 制作料酒剩下的酒糟经过加工就成为烹调用的糟，糟具有同料酒同样的调味作用。

Steaming with distillers'grains sauce (*zao*): Distillers'grains, which are left over from liquor making, are processed into a spicy agent for cooking that has the same function as the cooking wine.

五香料： 大料、茴香、桂皮、甘草、丁香(丁香花蕾)五种香料

混合为五香料，研成粉为五香粉。

Five Spices (*wu xiang liao*): A mixture of powdered star anise, fennel seed, cinnamon bark, licorice root and clove buds. Also referred to as the "five-powdered spices".

桂皮： 是桂树的皮，外皮粗糙呈现褐色。

Cinnamon (*gui pi*): The bark of cinnamon trees, brown in color.

料酒： 常用料酒是用糯米等粮食酿制成的，料酒，在烹调菜肴过程中起去腥、增香的作用，特别是烹制水产或肉类时少不了它。如没有料酒，可用适量的啤酒或白兰地代替，但没有料酒好。

Cooking wine (*liao jiu*): Cooking wine, brewed from grain, is applied to remove the fishy smell and increase the aroma of the dish. It is particularly essential when cooking dishes with aquatic ingredients and meat. While cooking wine is most desirable, in its absence, beer and brandy can be used.

勾芡： 勾芡就是在菜肴接近成熟时，将调好的湿淀粉加入锅内，搅拌均匀，使卤汁稠浓。增加卤汁对主料的附着力的一种方法。

Thickening with mixture of cornstarch and water (*gou qian*): When the dish is nearly cooked, put a previously prepared mixture of cornstarch and water into the dish and stir well so as to thicken the sauce or broth. This process promotes the flavored sauce to stay with the main materials of the dish.

勾芡作用： 1、增加菜肴汤汁的粘性和浓度。2、增加菜肴的光泽。

Major functions of this process: (1) Increase the stickiness and thickness of the sauce of the dish. (2) Making the dish look more shiny.

勾芡关键： 1、勾芡必须在菜肴即将成熟时候进行。2、勾芡时锅中汤汁不可太多或太少。3、必须在菜肴的口味、颜色已经调准后进行。4、勾芡时锅中油不宜太多。

Key for using this process: (1) This process must be conducted when the cooking of the dish is nearly complete. (2) The sauce in the wok must not be too much or too little when this thickening technique is applied. (3) This process can only be done after all efforts for flavoring and coloring of the dish are completed. (4) When doing the thickening process, the wok should not have too much oil in it.

如何使用筷子

吃中式饭菜一般使用筷子。筷子是用木或竹、骨及其它材料制成长 25-30 厘米、上方（各边为 8 毫米）下圆（直径为 3-5 毫米）的二根小棍。

使用时须依靠拇指及食指、中指和无名指的连贯配合。方法是：首先把两根筷子拿在右手，用食指、中指及无名指在距筷子近上端处各夹一根筷子，再把拇指和食指合在一起，如图 1。用筷子取食时，把食指和中指夹的一根向上抬，另一根不动，使两根筷子张开。如图 2。夹取食物时，把食指和中指夹的筷子往下压，夹住食物，抬起筷子进食，如图 3。

How to Use Chopsticks

Chopsticks for eating Chinese food are usually made from wood, bamboo, animal bones or other materials. About 25 to 30

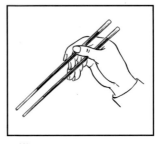

(1)

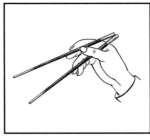

(2)

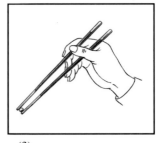

(3)

centimeters long, their top is square, about 0.8 square centimeter, and the low end round with a diameter of 3 to 5 millimeters.

The correct way of using the chopsticks requires concerted efforts of the thumb, index finger, middle finger and third finger. Hold the pair of chopsticks in the right hand, using the index finger, middle and third fingers to keep the chopsticks steady near their top and then push them open by moving the thumb and index finger. (See Drawing 1)

To pick things up with chopsticks, lift upward one of the two chopsticks with the index and middle fingers while keeping the other one where it is so as to separate the two. (See Drawing 2)

Once the chopsticks have picked up the food, press one of the chopsticks with the thumb and index finger and raise the pair. (See Drawing 3)

笼屉　蒸锅
Steaming tray(Long ti) Usually made of bamboo or wood,these often come in several tiers

炒锅
Skillet

火锅
Hot-pot

砂锅
Earthen pot

汤勺　炒铲　漏勺
Soup spoon Shovel Perforated spoon

筷子
Chopsticks

菜（面）板
Chopping board

菊花鱼段

主料：草鱼鱼肉 350 克。

调料：盐 4 克、糖 150 克、番茄酱 100 克、香醋 60 克、清汤 75 克、淀粉 500 克（实耗 200 克）、湿淀粉 15 克、麻油 10 克、油 1000 克（实耗 100 克）。

制作：①取斩去头、尾、剔除骨、刺的鱼肉，将鱼皮朝下放在砧板上，用刀斜切至鱼皮，每刀间相距 6 毫米，每隔 4 刀切断，将鱼块旋转 90 度，用刀直剔至鱼皮，每刀相距 6 毫米。（切成每边 6 毫米的菱形）。然后蘸上淀粉，再抖去余粉，即成菊花鱼生坯，待用。

②锅烧热，倒入油，烧至八成熟时，将菊花鱼生坯放入油锅，炸至金黄色，捞出装盘。锅内留余油 20 克，加清汤、糖、番茄酱、盐、搅匀，烧沸后，倒入香醋，用湿淀粉勾芡，淋入麻油出锅，倒在菊花鱼上即成。

特点：色泽金黄，形似菊花

口味：香脆松软，甜酸适口

Deep-fried Fish in the Shape of a Chrysanthemum

Ingredients:

1 freshwater fish（preferably grass carp）about 350 grams（0.77lb）

4 grams（2/3tsp）salt

150 grams（11.5tbsp）sugar

100 grams（5.5tbsp）ketchup

60 grams（4tbsp）vinegar

75 grams（5tbsp）water

500 grams（1.1lb）dry cornstarch（only 200 grams or 0.44lb to be actually consumed）

15 grams（1tbsp）mixture of cornstarch and water

10 grams（2tsp）sesame oil

1,000grams（4cups）cooking oil（only 100grams or 8tbsp to be actually consumed）

Directions:

(1)First remove the fish's head, tail and bones to obtain two large chunks of meat. Put the meat on a chopping board with skin side down. Make slanting cuts deep into the skin with a 6 mm-space between every two cuts. Section the fish with every four cuts. Turn the fish around 90 degrees and use the chopper to cut in a vertical manner right to the skin with 6 mm（0.23 in）between every two cuts to create diamond shapes of about 6mm（0.23 in）on each side. Spread dry cornstarch on the fish. Dust off unnecessary cornstarch and the chunks will show a preliminary chrysanthemum shape.

(2)Put the cooking oil in the wok and heat it until it is about 200-220℃（390-430℉）. Deep-fry the ready cut fish chunks until they are golden brown. Put the fried fish on a plate. Now pour out most of the oil but leave about 20 grams（1.5tbsp）of it in the wok for making sauce. Add in the water, sugar, ketchup, salt and mix well. When the sauce is boiling, put in the vinegar and then the cornstarch-water mixture to make the sauce into thick gravy. Add in the sesame oil and immediately pour the gravy onto the fried fish on the plate.

Features: When cooked, the fish is in golden color and chrysanthemum shape.

Taste: Crispy, soft, sweet and sour to the right degree.

菊花鱼段

Deep-fride Fish in the Shape of a Chrysanthemum

三丝鱼卷

主料：草鱼鱼肉 100 克。

辅料：冬笋 30 克、香菇 25 克、火腿肉 25 克。

调料：青葱 3 克、鸡蛋清 1 只、淀粉 10 克、盐 3 克、味精 1 克、湿淀粉 25 克,油 25 克,清汤 100 克。

制作：①将斩去头、尾、剔除骨、刺的鱼肉，鱼皮向下放在砧板上，沿着断面 3 毫米处一刀切至鱼皮，再一刀切断，成为长约 3 厘米、宽约 6 毫米的夹刀片（第一刀不切断，第二刀切断，称夹刀片），放在盆中加鸡蛋清，盐 2 克，味精 0.5 克，淀粉 10 克拌匀上浆备用。火腿肉洗净煮熟。

②将冬笋、香菇、熟火腿、葱分别切成 3 厘米左右长的细丝，将鱼片横向，鱼皮向上，平摊在砧板上，放上各种丝，卷成鱼卷，排在盘中，加油 5 克，上笼水开后，蒸 5 分钟。

③将蒸好的鱼卷排放在盘中，将锅烧热，放油 20 克、盐 1 克、味精 0.5 克，清汤 100 克，烧沸后放湿淀粉 5 克勾芡，浇在鱼卷上即可。

特点：色泽洁白，形似兰花

口味：肉质细嫩，味道鲜美

Fish Rolls

Ingredients：

100 grams (0.22lb) freshwater fish (preferably grass carp) meat

30 grams (1.1oz) fresh bamboo shoots

25 grams (0.7oz) mushrooms

25 grams (0.7oz) ham

3 grams (0.1oz) scallions

1 egg white

10 grams (1.5tbsp) dry cornstarch

3 grams (1/2tsp) salt

1 gram (1/4tsp) monosodium glutamate (MSG) (See Glossary for an alternative ingredient)

25 gram (1.5tbsp) mixture of cornstarch and water

10 grams (2tsp) oil

100 grams (6tbsp) water

Directions：

(1) First remove the fish's head, tail and bones. Then put the remainder of the fish on the chopping board with the skin side down and, starting from about 3 cm (1.2in) from the end, cut the fish into fillets of about 3cm (1.2in) long and 6 mm (0.23 in) wide. Put the fish into the batter of egg white, 2 grams (1/3tsp) of salt, 0.5 gram (1/8tsp) of MSG and 10 grams (1.5tbsp) of cornstarch. Boil the ham until it is done.

(2) Cut the bamboo shoots, mushrooms, ham and scallions into thin shreds of 3 cm (1.2in) long. Arrange the fish chunks on the chopping board in a horizontal way and, with the fish skin on the top side, spread the shreds and roll into fish rolls. Put the rolls on a plate, spread 5 grams (1tsp) of oil over them and steam for 5 minutes after the water reaches boiling point.

(3) Put the steamed fish rolls on a plate. Heat the wok and put in 20 grams (1.5tbsp) of oil, 1 gram (1/6tsp) of salt, 0.5 gram (1/8tsp) of MSG and 100 grams (6tbsp) of water. When the soup starts to boil, put in 5 grams (1tbsp) of the cornstarch-water mixture to thicken the soup and then spread the gravy on the fish rolls.

Features: The dish is white in color and looks like magnolia flowers.

Taste: The meat is tender and delicious.

三丝鱼卷
Fish Rolls

芝麻鱼条

主料：草鱼鱼肉 250 克（最好选用没有小鱼骨的鱼）

辅料：白芝麻 50 克、鸡蛋 2 个。

调料：料酒 10 克、盐 3 克、咖喱粉 0.5 克，葱、姜末各 10 克、味精 1 克、油 200 克（实耗 50 克），淀粉 50 克，辣酱油一小碟。

制作：①取去除头、尾、骨、刺和皮的鱼肉，切成 1 厘米厚的片，再顺丝切成长约 4 厘米，宽 1 厘米的鱼条，加盐、味精、咖喱粉，及葱、姜末拌匀，腌渍约 15 分钟。

②将鸡蛋打散，边打边加入干淀粉，调成蛋粉糊，将腌渍过的鱼条挂上蛋粉糊后，两面拍上白芝麻，抖去没粘住的芝麻，成芝麻鱼条生坯。

③锅置旺火上烧热，倒入油，油温升至六成热时，改小火，将鱼条逐个炸至熟后，捞出装盘，随带辣酱油 1 小碟上席。

特点：色泽金黄

口味：外酥里嫩

Fish Steak with Sesame

Ingredients：

250 grams（0.55lb）fish meat（freshwater fish without small bones such as grass carp recommended）50 grams（0.11lb）white sesame 2 eggs 10 grams（2tsp）cooking wine 3 grams（1/2tsp）salt 0.5 gram（1/4tsp）curry 10 gram（0.35oz）finely cut scallions 10 gram（0.35oz）finely cut ginger 1 gram（1/4tsp）MSG 200 grams（4/5 cup）cooking oil（only 50 grams or 4tbsp to be actually consumed）50 grams（8tbsp）dry cornstarch1 small plate chilli oil

Directions：

(1) Remove the head, tail, bones and skin of the fish and cut into slices of 1 cm（0.39 in）thick, then cut along the grain into fillets 4 cm（1.6in）long and 1 cm wide. Put the fillets into the mix of salt, MSG, curry, scallions and ginger and let them marinate for 15 minutes.

(2) Beat the eggs while adding in dry cornstarch to make a paste. Coat the prepared fish fillets with the paste. Spread sesame seeds on both sides of the fillets, shake off those that do not stick to the fillets.

(3) Heat the wok with a hot fire, pour in oil until it is around 135-170℃（275-340℉）. Turn the fire to low and one by one deep-fry the fillets until they are fully cooked. Place them on a plate and serve together with the small plate of chilli oil.

Features：The fillets are golden in color.

Taste：Crispy outside and tender inside.

芝麻鱼条
Fish Steak with Sesame

青椒鱼丝

主料：草鱼鱼肉 300 克。

辅料：青椒 30 克。

调料：鸡蛋清 1 只、料酒 10 克、盐 5 克、油 50 克、淀粉 5 克、清汤 25 克、湿淀粉 5 克、味精 1 克、麻油 3 克。

制作：①将除去头、尾、骨、刺和鱼皮的鱼肉洗净滤干，切成长 7 厘米，宽 0.4 厘米的丝，放盐 2 克，鸡蛋清 1 只，淀粉 5 克上浆备用。用刀把青椒剖开除去籽和蒂再切成丝。把清汤、料酒、味精、盐 1 克，湿淀粉合成卤汁，待用。

②旺火热锅，倒入油 40 克，油温升至六成热时，倒入鱼丝滑炒开，断生即倒出，原锅加油 10 克，倒入青椒丝炒一下，再入卤汁，然后把鱼丝倒入翻炒均匀入味，淋麻油出锅、装盘即成。

特点：色泽白绿相间

口味：肉质细嫩，味道鲜美

注：鱼除去中段，剩下的部分，可以做鱼汤，做到一鱼二吃。

Fish Shreds with Green Peppers

Ingredients：

300 grams (0.66lb) freshwater fish (preferably grass carp) meat

30 grams (1.1oz) green peppers

1 egg white

10 grams (2tsp) cooking wine

5 grams (5/6tsp) salt

50 grams (4tbsp) cooking oil

5 grams (1tbsp) cornstarch

25 grams (1.6tbsp) water

5 grams (1tsp) mixture of cornstarch and water

1 gram (1/4tsp) MSG

3 grams (3/5tsp) sesame oill

Directions：

(1) Wash the headless, tailless and boneless fish, and leave the meat to drain. When it is dry, cut the fish into shreds about 7 cm (2.7in) long and 0.4 cm (0.16 in) wide. Put the mixture of 2 grams (1/3tsp) of salt, 1 egg white and 5 grams (1tbsp) of cornstarch on the shreds. Cut the green peppers open, remove the seeds and stem and cut the peppers into slices. Prepare a sauce of water, cooking wine, MSG, 1 gram (1/6tsp) of salt and the cornstarch-water mixture and leave it aside for the time being.

(2) Heat the wok on a hot fire and pour in 40 grams (3tbsp) of cooking oil. Heat until the mixture is about 135-170℃ (275-340℉). Quick stir-fry the fish shreds and take them out when they are still rare. Add in 10 grams (2tsp) of cooking oil and quick stir-fry the pepper slices. Pour in the previously prepared sauce and add in the fish shreds. Turn and mix them in the wok. Spread the sesame oil over the fish and put it and peppers on a plate to serve.

Features：The dish shows mixed colors of white and green.

Taste：The fish shreds have a tender quality and are delicious in taste.

Note：Apart from the middle section of the fish used to cook this dish, the other parts that have been cut off can be used to make fish soup to produce two dishes with one fish.

青椒鱼丝
Fish Shreds with Green Peppers

松仁鱼米

主料：草鱼鱼肉 500 克。

辅料：松子仁 50 克。

调料：盐 6 克、味精 1 克、葱段、姜片各 20 克、辣椒 2 克、料酒 10 克、油 60 克、鸡蛋清 1 只、湿淀粉 10 克、清汤 25 克、淀粉 10 克。

制作：①将除去头、尾、骨、刺和皮的鱼肉切成 2 毫米厚的片，再顺丝切成 2 毫米宽的鱼丝，再把鱼丝横切成松子大小的鱼米，放盐 2 克，鸡蛋清 1 只，湿淀粉 10 克上浆备用。把辣椒切成如鱼米大小。

②锅内放油 50 克，烧热后放入松子仁炸熟，取出装备冷却。

③旺火热锅，油温升至 5 成熟时倒入鱼米，滑炒至熟，倒出装盘，锅内留余油 10 克加热，放葱、姜、辣椒米略炒几下，加料酒、清汤、盐 4 克，味精 1 克，倒入松子仁、鱼米翻炒，加湿淀粉勾芡，淋油即成。

特点：色泽洁白

口味：咸鲜中带微辣，具有松仁香味

Fish Cubes with Pine Nuts

Ingredients：

500 grams（1.1lb）freshwater fish（preferably grass carp）meat
50 grams（0.11lb）pine nuts
6 grams（1tsp）salt
1 gram（1/4tsp）MSG
20 grams（0.7oz）scallions
20 grams（0.7oz）ginger slices
2 grams（0.07oz）hot chilli
10 grams（2tsp）cooking wine
60 grams（4.5tbsp）cooking oil
1 egg white
10 grams（1.5tsp）mixture of cornstarch and water
25 grams（1.6tbsp）water
10 grams（1.5tbsp）dry cornstarch

Directions：

(1) Cut the headless, tailless, boneless and skinless fish into slices 2 mm（0.08 in）thick and cut along the grain into shreds of 2 mm width. The shreds are further cut cross ways into small cubes the size of pine nuts. Make a batter of 2 grams（1/3tsp）of salt, 1 egg white and 10 grams of（1.5tbsp）cornstarch-water mixture to marinate the fish cubes. Cut the hot chillies into the size of the fish cubes.

(2) Pour 50 grams（4tbsp）of oil into the wok and when the oil is hot, throw in the pine nut kernels and deep-fry them until they are well done. Take them out and put them on a plate to cool off.

(3) Use a hot fire to heat the oil in the wok to about 110-135℃（230-275℉）. Put in the fish cubes and stir-fry. Put them on a plate and leave 10 grams（2tsp）of oil in the wok to further heat. Throw in the scallion shreds, ginger and chilli and quickly stir-fry. Add in the cooking wine, water, 4 grams（2/3tsp）of salt and 1 gram（1/4tsp）of MSG. Also put in the pine nuts and fish cubes to stir-fry. Add in the cornstarch-water mixture and spread some more oil on top of the ingredients and the dish is done.

Features：The color is pure white.

Taste: It tastes salty and refreshing but has a slight spicy flavor. It also has the fragrance of pine nuts.

松仁鱼米
Fish Cubes with Pine Nuts

炸鱼排

主料：草鱼鱼肉 350 克。

调料：淀粉 100 克、盐 5 克、味精 1 克、鸡蛋一只、油 500 克（实耗 100 克）料酒 10 克。

制作：①用刀将去头、尾、剔除骨、刺和鱼皮的鱼肉切成厚 0.5 厘米的大片。

②将料酒、味精、盐同鱼片一起，拌匀后，腌渍半小时，然后打入鸡蛋搅均，取出每片拍上淀粉备用。

③旺火热锅，锅中放油，待油温升至七成热时，投入鱼片炸至金黄色捞出装盘,蘸椒盐或番茄酱蘸食。

特点:色泽金黄

口味:外脆里嫩, 鱼肉鲜美

Deep-fried Fish Fillets

Ingredients：

350 grams (0.77lb)freshwater fish (preferably grass carp)

100 grams (0.22lb)dry cornstarch

5 grams (5/6tsp)salt

1 gram (1/4tsp)MSG

1 egg

500 grams (2 cups)cooking oil (only 100 grams or 8tbsp to be actually consumed)

10 grams (2tsp)cooking wine

Directions：

(1)Cut the headless, tailless, boneless and skinless fish into large slices of about 0.5 cm (0.2in)thickness.

(2)Mix the cooking wine, MSG and salt with the fish slices and let the mixture rest for half an hour.Crack the egg and mix fish in the yolk.Then spread the cornstarch on the fish slices.

(3)Use a hot fire to heat the oil in the wok to about 180-200℃ (355-390℉), put in the fish slices and deep-fry them until they are golden brown in color.Put them on a plate to be served either with pepper salt or tomato sauce.

Features：They have a nice golden color.

Taste：They are crispy outside and tender inside.

炸鱼排
Deep-fried Fish Fillets

龙井鱼片

主料：草鱼鱼片 300 克。

辅料：龙井茶叶（其它绿菜也可）1 克。

调料：鸡蛋清 1 只、清汤 50 克、料酒 10 克、盐 5 克、味精 1 克、湿淀粉 20 克，油 250 克，淀粉 10 克。

制作：①取去头、尾，除去骨、刺和皮的鱼肉，切成厚约 0.3 毫米，长 5 厘米、宽 4 厘米左右的片。

②用鸡蛋清、盐 2 克，淀粉同鱼片一起上浆备用。茶叶用 50 克沸水泡开后去水，留茶叶待用。

③旺火热锅，锅内加油，待油温升至 5 成熟时，改中火，投入鱼片滑炒至熟，倒出。锅内加余油 10 克烧热，倒入清汤，味精、盐 3 克，调好味，勾芡，倒入鱼片、茶叶翻炒，淋油出锅装盘即可。

特点：茶叶清香，色泽悦目

口味：肉质鲜嫩

Dragon Well Fish Slices

Ingredients:

300 grams (0.66lb) of freshwater fish (preferably grass carp) slices

1 gram (1tsp) Dragon Well Tea (or other kind of green tea)

1 egg white

50 grams (3tbsp) water

10 grams (2tsp) cooking wine

5 grams (5/6tsp) salt

1 gram (1/4tsp) MSG

20 grams (1tbsp) cornstarch-water mixture

250 grams (1 cup) cooking oil

10 grams (1.5tbsp) dry cornstarch

Directions:

(1) Cut the headless, tailless, boneless and skinless fish into slices of about 3 mm (0.12 in) thick, 5 cm (2 in) long and 4 cm (1.5in) wide.

(2) Apply the mixture of the egg white, 2 grams (1/3tsp) of salt and cornstarch onto the fish slices. Put 50 grams (3tbsp) of hot water into a pot to boil the tea, pour out the water and keep the tea leaves for later use.

(3) Use a hot fire to heat the oil in the wok to about 110-135℃ (230-275℉). Now change to a medium fire, throw in the fish slices and stir-fry them. Then move them onto a plate. Heat 10 grams (2tsp) of oil in the wok, add in the water, MSG, and 3 grams (1/2tsp) of salt. Add the mixture of cornstarch and water to thicken the sauce. Put in the fish slices and tea leaves to stir-fry. Spread some sesame oil in the wok and put the dish on a plate to serve.

Features: The tea leaves give a refreshing and fragrant taste and add color to the delightful dish.

Taste: The meat is very tender.

龙井鱼片
Dragon Well Fish Slices

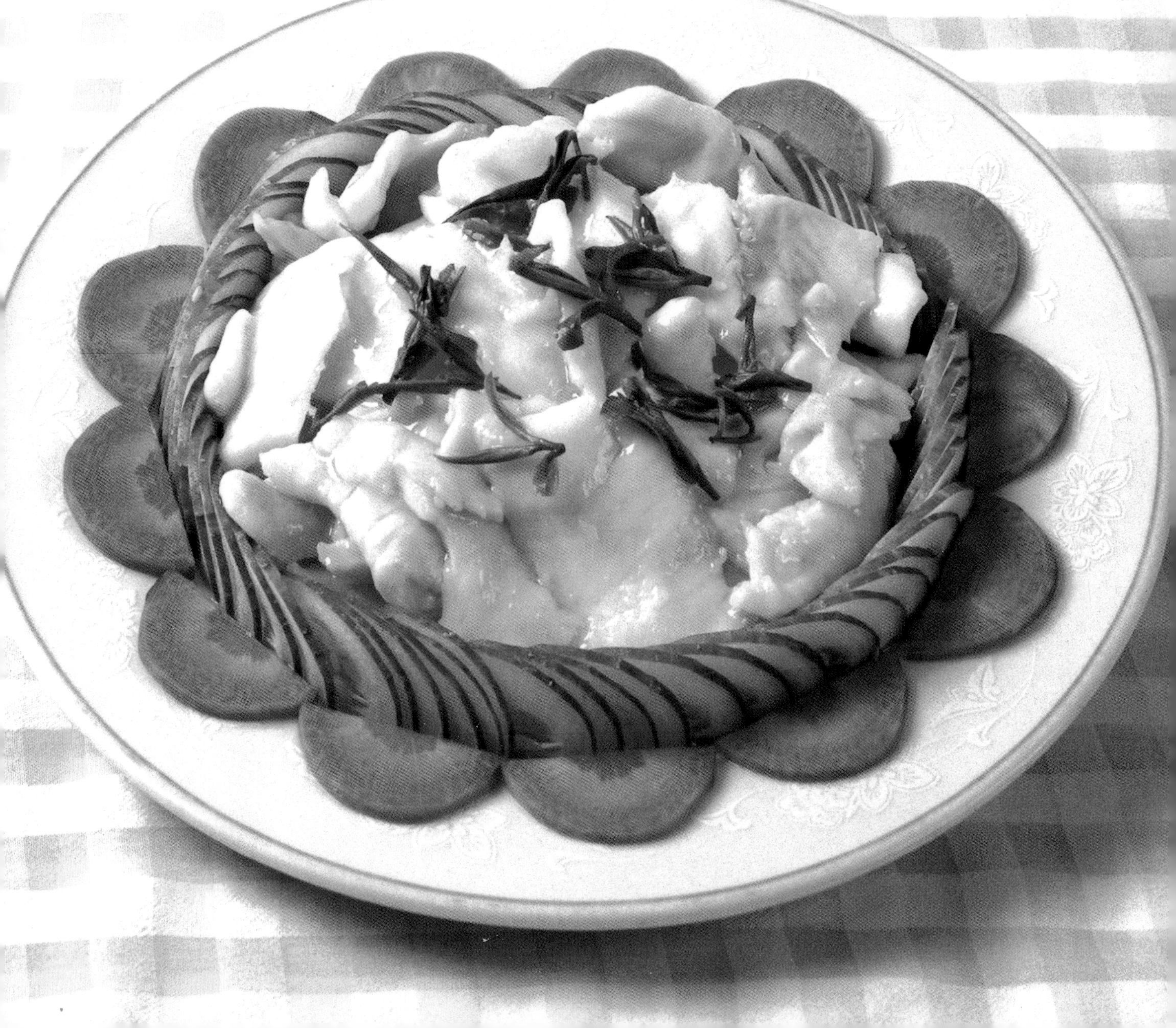

二丝鱼条

主料：草鱼鱼肉 300 克。

辅料：熟笋 25 克、熟火腿 25 克、青椒 25 克。

调料：料酒 20 克，盐 4 克，味精 1 克，湿淀粉 20 克，麻油 5 克，油 75 克，鸡蛋清 1 个，胡椒粉 2 克，淀粉 10 克。

制作：①将剔出骨、刺、除去皮的鱼肉切成长约 4 厘米，宽、厚各 1 厘米的鱼条，加料酒 10 克，盐 3 克，淀粉、鸡蛋清上浆备用。

②将笋、火腿、青椒切成比鱼条略小的条备用。

③旺火热锅，放入油 50 克待油温升至五成热时改中火，将鱼条下锅滑炒至熟，倒出。

④锅内放油 25 克，放放火腿、青椒、笋条翻炒几下后，倒入熟的鱼条加盐 2 克，味精、料酒 10 克，炒熟后用湿淀粉勾芡，淋上麻油出锅装盘即成。

特点：色彩斑斓

口味：咸鲜

Fish with Bamboo and Ham Shreds

Ingredients:

300 grams (0.66lb) freshwater fish (preferably grass carp) meat
25 grams (0.9oz) boiled bamboo shoots
25 grams (0.9oz) ham
25 grams (0.9oz) green peppers steamed
20 grams (4tsp) cooking wine
4 grams (2/3tsp) salt
1 gram (1/4tsp) MSG
20 grams (1tbsp) mixture of cornstarch and water
5 grams (1tsp) sesame oil
75 grams (4tbsp) cooking oil
1 egg white
1 gram (1/2tsp) ground pepper
10 grams (1.5tbsp) dry cornstarch

Directions:

(1) Cut the boneless and skinless fish meat into slices of 4 cm (1.5-1.6 in) in length and width and 1 cm (0.39 in) in thickness. Marinate it with the batter of 10 grams (3tsp) of cooking wine, 3 grams (1/2tsp) of salt, the cornstarch and egg white.

(2) Cut bamboo shoots, ham and green peppers into shreds smaller than the fish slices.

(3) Heat the wok on a hot fire, pour in 50 grams (4tbsp) of cooking oil and, when it is about 110-135°C (230-275°F), turn the fire to medium and put in the fish slices in to stir-fry. When the slices are done, put them into a plate.

(4) Keep 25 grams (2tbsp) of oil in the wok and put in the ham, green peppers and bamboo shoots to stir-fry for a few seconds. Then add in the fish slices, 2 grams (1/3tsp) of salt, MSG and 10 grams (2tsp) of cooking wine. When all the slices are done, add in the cornstarch-water mixture, spread the sesame oil and serve.

Features: This is a very colorful dish.
Taste: Salty and succulent to the right degree.

Fish with Bamboo and Ham Shreds

油淋鱼（瓦块）

主料：草鱼鱼肉 400 克。

辅料：香菜 30 克。

调料：油 250 克（实耗 75 克）、葱末 3 克、姜末 3 克、蒜 5 克、酱油 100 克、辣酱油 20 克、糖 20 克、味精 0.5 克、胡椒粉 1 克、盐 3 克、料酒 25 克、淀粉 500 克（实耗 200 克）、清汤 75 克。

制作：①取除去骨、刺的鱼肉，将鱼皮朝上放在贴板上，斜刀切成宽的 6 毫米的夹刀片，加料酒、盐、腌渍 10 分钟。

②将腌渍过的鱼片拍上淀粉，抖去余粉备用。

③将香菜拣洗干净，切成长 6 毫米的段。

④旺火热锅放油待油温升至七成热时，放入备好的鱼片炸至金黄色，倒出滤油。

⑤原锅留余油 20 克放葱姜末煸炒出香味后放清汤、酱油、辣酱油、糖、味精、胡椒粉，烧沸后投入香菜浇在鱼肉上，即成。

特点：形似瓦片

口味：外脆里嫩、甜中带辣

Oil-sprinkled Fish Chunks (Tile-shaped Fried Fish)

Ingredients：

400 grams (0.88lb) freshwater fish (preferably grass carp) meat

30 grams (1.1oz) coriander

250 grams (1 cup) cooking oil (only 75 grams or 6tbsp to actually be consumed)

3 grams (0.1oz) finely cut scallions

3 grams (0.1oz) finely chopped ginger

5 grams (0.18oz) garlic

100 grams (5.5tbsp) soy sauce

20 grams (1tbsp) hot spicy soy sauce

20 grams (1.5tbsp) sugar

0.5 gram (1/8tsp) MSG

1 gram (1/2tsp) ground pepper

3 grams (1/2tsp) salt

25 grams (5tsp) cooking wine

500 grams (1.lb) dry cornstarch (only 200 grams or 0.44lb to actually be consumed)

75 grams (5tbsp) water

Directions：

(1) Place boneless fish on the chopping board with the skin side on top. Cut in a slanting way into chunks 6 mm (0.23 in) long each, with another cut to skin depth at the 3 mm (0.12 in) point. Put the fish chunks in cooking wine and salt to marinate for 10 minutes.

(2) Dust the cornstarch on the marinated fish.

(3) Wash the coriander and cut it into sections of 6 mm (0.23 in) in length.

(4) Heat the oil in the wok with a hot fire until it is about 180-200℃ (355-390℉). Put in the fish chunks to deep-fry until they are golden brown in color. Then drain off the oil.

(5) Keep 20 grams (1.5tbsp) of oil in the wok. Put in the scallions and ginger and stir-fry until they give a nice smell. Now put in the water, soy sauce, spicy soy sauce, sugar, MSG and ground pepper to stew. When the soup reaches a boiling point, spread the coriander on top of the fish and the dish is done.

Features: The fish chunks resemble the shape of tiles and thus the other name for the dish.

Taste: Crispy on the surface but tender inside, with a slight spicy taste.

油淋鱼（瓦块）
Oil-sprinkled Fish Chunks (Tile-shaped Fried Fish)

凤尾鱼

主料：小鳜鱼 3 条（共约 250 克）

辅料：火腿丝、葱丝、姜丝、胡萝卜丝、笋丝各 10 克。

调料：盐 3 克、味精 1 克、料酒 5 克、清汤 50 克、湿淀粉 25 克、淀粉 10 克、油 250 克（实耗 50 克）、鸡蛋清 1 只。

制作：①将鱼洗杀干净，皆切下头，用刀贴着鱼背脊骨横切至鱼尾，用手把半片不带背骨的鱼肉拉下，要连着半片尾巴。用同样的方法切取下另外的半片鱼肉下，再用刀沿着肋骨侧线割去肋骨。

②在每片鱼肉厚的地方划两刀，但不能破皮，放蛋清、盐 2 克，湿淀粉上浆备用。

③旺火热锅放入油，油温升至三成热时，放入鱼肉，改小火焐熟，倒出滤油，装盘。

④锅内留余油 25 克，放入辅料和盐 1 克，味精、料酒、清汤，调好口味，用湿淀粉勾芡，出锅浇在鱼身上即可。

特点：色形具佳。

口味：咸鲜适口，肉肥嫩

Phoenix Tail Fish

Ingredients：

3 small freshwater manderin fish (about 250 grams or 0.55lb together)

10 grams (0.36oz) each of ham, scallions, ginger, carrots and bamboo shoots, all cut into shreds

3 grams (1/2tsp) salt

1 gram (1/4tsp) MSG

5 grams (1tsp) cooking wine

50 grams (3tbsp) water

25 grams (1.5tbsp) mixture of cornstarch and water

10 grams (1.5tbsp) dry cornstarch

250 grams (1 cup) cooking oil (only 50 grams or 4tbsp to be actually consumed)

1 egg white

Directions：

(1) Cut the heads of the fish off, then cut along each spine to the tail. Separate the two halves of each fish to expose the bones while keeping the tail intact. Remove the ribs.

(2) Make two slash cuts where the meat is thick without breaking the skin. Marinate the fish in egg white, 2 grams (1/3tsp) of salt and cornstarch-water mixture.

(3) Heat the oil with a hot fire until it is about 50-60℃ (120-140℉). Put in the fish and stew with low fire. When it is done, put the fish on a plate.

(4) Keep 25 grams (2tbsp) of oil in the wok and throw in the ingredients, including 1 gram (1/6tsp) of salt, MSG, cooking wine and water. Thicken it with cornstarch-water mixture and then pour the gravy on the fish.

Features：It is delicious and looks inviting.

Taste：Tasty and the meat is tender.

清蒸鱼

主料：鲳鱼一条约 250 克。

辅料：笋片 4 片、火腿 4 片、香菇 4 个。

调料：料酒 10 克、盐 3 克、葱段 4 克、姜片 5 克、味精 1 克、油 10 克、清水 200 克。

制作：①鱼宰杀后去鳞、鳃及内脏，清洗干净，在鱼身两面肉厚处剞上"十"字花刀。

②锅内放入清水 200 克，烧沸后，把鱼投入，1 分钟后，即捞出，用清水洗去血沫。

③将鱼平放在盘中，在两面抹上料酒、盐、味精和油。再放上香菇、笋片、火腿片、葱、姜上笼蒸 10 分钟左右，去葱、姜，装盘即成。

特点：肉质鲜嫩

口味：咸鲜

Steamed Fish

Ingredients：
1 seawater butterfish about 250 grams (0.55lb)
4 bamboo shoot slices
4 ham slices
4 mushrooms
10 grams (2tsp) cooking wine
3 grams (1/2tsp) salt
4 grams (0.14oz) scallion sectione
5 grams (0.18oz) ginger sliced
1 gram (1/4tsp) MSG
10 grams (2tsp) cooking oil
200 grams (4/5 cup) water

Directions：
(1) Gut the fish and wash it clean. Make slashes in the shape of a cross where the meat is thick.

(2) Heat the water and, when it is boiling, put the fish in and boil it for 1 minute. Wash off the blood stains on the fish body with clean water.

(3) Put the fish on a plate. Apply the cooking wine, salt, MSG and oil to both sides of the fish. Put in the mushrooms, bamboo shoots, ham slices, scallions and ginger and steam for 10 minutes. Remove the scallions and ginger and now serve.

Features：The meat has a tender quality.
Taste：Salty and refreshing to the taste.

清蒸鱼
Steamed Fish

椒盐鱼

主料：鲳鱼一条约 250 克。

辅料：生菜 1 棵、红辣椒 1 只。

调料：葱段、姜片各 5 克、料酒 25 克、盐 2 克，麻油 25 克、油 100 克、椒盐 3 克。

制作：① 鱼宰杀后去鳞、鳃、内脏，洗净，两面剞上"十"字花刀，放入盘中，抹盐、料酒，鱼肚中塞入葱段、姜片放在冰箱中腌渍 1 小时。红辣椒切丝。

② 旺火热锅，放入油加热至七成，改中火，将腌好的鱼去掉葱姜，投入油锅中、煎至两香酥金黄色，放入红椒丝，半分钟后捞出。

③ 把煎好的鱼放入垫有生菜的盘中，撒上椒盐，淋上烧热的麻油即可。

特点：色泽金黄

口味：外酥里嫩，味鲜美

Fish with Pepper Salt

Ingredients：
1 seawater butterfish about 250 grams（0.55lb）in weight
some lettuce leaves
1 red chilli
5 grams (0.9oz) each of sectioned scallions and sliced ginger
25 grams (5tsp)cooking wine
2 grams (1/3tsp)salt
25 grams (2tbsp)sesame oil
100 grams (8tbsp)cooking oil
3 grams (1tsp) pepper salt

Directions：
(1)Gut the fish and make cuts in the shape of crosses where the meat is thick. Put the fish in a plate and apply salt and cooking wine. Stuff it with sectioned scallions and ginger slices and leave the fish in the refrigerator for an hour. Cut the hot chilli into shreds.

(2)Heat the wok with oil over a hot fire and turn the fire down to medium after the oil reaches about 180-200℃ (350-390℉). Put the marinated fish in the wok to deep-fry. When the fish shows a golden color, put in the chilli shreds. Take it out in just half a minute.

(3) Put the deep-fried fish on a plate already with lettuce leaves in it. Spread the pepper salt and sprinkle sesame oil.

Features：Beautiful golden color.
Taste：Crispy outside and tender and delicious inside.

椒盐鱼
Fish with Pepper Salt

煎封鱼

主料：鲳鱼 750 克。

调料：酱油 20 克、姜汁 15 克（姜 10 克用刀拍碎后加清水至 15 克就浸泡而成）、料酒 10 克、葱花 2 克、蒜茸 1 克、姜末 1 克、麻油 2 克、胡椒粉 0.5 克、油 250 克（实耗 50 克左右）、煎封汁 250 克（煎封汁：清汤 100 克，鸡汁 75 克，酱油 5 克，糖 3 克，盐 2 克，味精 0.5 克，混合煮沸即可）。

制作：①将鱼洗杀干净，用刀在鱼身两边斜剞数刀，用酱油，姜汁腌渍 15 分钟备用。

②旺火烧锅倒入油，待油温升至 6 成热时投入鱼煎至两面酱红色，捞出滤油，锅内余油 25 克，放葱花、蒜茸、姜末、胡椒粉，炒出香味后，倒入煎封汁和鱼，放入料酒，烧沸后 2 分钟淋麻油出锅，装盘。

特点：色泽酱红，具有特殊香味

口味：鲜香，肉质细嫩

Deep-fried Fish in Mixed Sauce

Ingredients：
750 grams (1.65lb) seawater butterfish
20 grams (1tbsp) soy sauce
15 grams (1tbsp) ginger juice (Crush 10 grams or 0.36oz of ginger with the side of a chopper and soak it in 15 grams or 1tbsp of water)
10 grams (2tsp) cooking wine
2 grams (0.07oz) finely cut scallions
1 gram (0.035oz) crushed garlic
1 gram (0.035oz) minced ginger
2 grams (2/5tsp) sesame oil
0.5 gram (1/4tsp) ground pepper
250 grams (1 cup) cooking oil (only 50 grams or 4tbsp to be actually consumed)
250 grams (14tbsp) mixed sauce (100 grams or 6tbsp water, 75 grams or 5tbsp chicken broth, 5 grams or 1tsp soy sauce, 3 grams or 2/3tsp sugar, 2 grams or 1/3tsp salt and 0.5 gram or 1/8tsp MSG mixed together and heat to boiling point)

Directions：
(1) Clean the fish and make several slanting cuts on both sides of the fish. Marinate it in soy sauce and ginger juice for 15 minutes.

(2) Heat the wok, put in the cooking oil. When the oil is heated to about 135-170℃ (275-340°F), put in the fish and deep-fry until it shows a dark red color on both sides. Remove it from the cooking oil. Pour out most of the oil but leave 25 grams (2tbsp) in the wok. Put in the scallions, crushed garlic and ginger and pepper, and stir-fry this until it gives out an aromatic smell. Put in the mixed sauce, fish and cooking wine. Sprinkle the sesame oil two minutes after the sauce starts boiling. It is now ready to serve.

Features: The fish is dark red in color and gives out a special fragrant smell.
Taste: Fragrant in smell and tender in texture.

煎封鱼
Deep-fried Fish in Mixed Sauce

干煎鱼

主料：带鱼 400 克。

辅料：生菜叶 3-4 张。

调料：葱花 30 克、姜片 25 克、料酒 25 克、盐 5 克、麻油 15 克、油 100 克。

制作：①鱼杀洗干净，去鳞、鳃，取出内脏滤干水份后，两面划平行直刀纹，刀纹相距 3 毫米左右，然后切成长约 6~7 厘米左右的段。

②将鱼放在盘中抹盐、料酒，撒入葱花、姜片，放入冰箱腌渍 1 小时左右。

③旺火热锅，放入油，油温升 6 成热时，放入腌渍好的鱼块，用中火，把鱼块煎至两成金黄香酥，捞出，放在垫有生菜的盘中，浇上烧热的麻油即可。

特点：色泽金黄

口味：鲜香

Braised Fish Fillets

Ingredients:

400 grams (0.88lb) freshwater fish

3-4 lettuce leaves

30 grams (1.1oz) finely cut scallions

25 grams (0.9oz) ginger slices

25 grams (5tsp) cooking wine

5 grams (5/6tsp) salt

15 grams (1tbsp) sesame oil

100 grams (8tbsp) cooking oil

Directions:

(1) Wash the fish clean, remove the scales, gills and gut it. Gently cut both sides of the fish horizontally with about 3 mm (0.12 in) space between each two cuts. Then section the fish into 6-7 cm (2.4-2.8 in) pieces.

(2) Put the fish on a plate, rub in salt and sprinkle cooking wine, scallions and ginger slices over it and leave it for about an hour in the refrigerator.

(3) Heat the oil to 135-170℃ (275-340°F), put in the marinated fish sections and deep-fry over a medium fire until the fish is golden brown in color on both sides. Remove the fish sections and place them on the lettuce leaves already arranged on a plate. Heat the sesame oil and spread it on the fish.

Features: Golden brown in color.

Taste: Refreshingly tasty.

干煎鱼
Braised Fish Fillets

椒盐虾

主料：虾 500 克。

调料：淀粉 35 克、椒盐 3 克、料酒 10 克、盐 4 克、油 250 克（实耗 100 克）。

制作：①将虾洗净，用刀在背部划开，剔去肠子，同盐、料酒一起放入盆中腌渍 15 分钟。

②旺火热锅，加油，待油温升至六成热时，将拍过淀粉的虾投入油锅中，炸至色红壳脆，捞出滤油。

③炒锅倒去余油，倒入炸过的虾，撒上椒盐，颠翻出锅装盘。

特点：色泽深红

口味：鲜嫩味美

Shrimps in Pepper Salt

Ingredients：

500 grams (1.1lb)shrimps

35 grams (1.25oz)dry cornstarch

3 grams (1/2tsp)pepper salt (See glossary for making this ingredient)

10 grams (2tsp)cooking wine

4 grams (2/3tsp)salt

250 grams (1 cup)of cooking oil (100 grams or 8tbsp to be actually consumed)

Directions：

(1)Wash the shrimps clean.Cut open their backs to remove the dark intestine.Marinate in salt and cooking wine for 15 minutes.

(2)Heat the oil in a wok to 135-170℃ (275-340℉).Put in the shrimps which have been dusted with dry cornstarch.Deep-fry until their shells are red.Take them out of the wok and drain off the oil.

(3)Pour oil out of the wok, put in the deep-fried shrimps, sprinkle with the pepper salt, quickly turn them and then place them on a plate.

Features：Red in color.

Taste：Tender and tasty.

椒盐虾
Shrimps in Peeper Salt

葱姜肉蟹

主料：肉蟹 600 克。

调料：葱段 5 克、姜片 5 克、料酒 25 克、盐 6 克、味精 1 克、油 25 克。

制作：①将肉蟹剥去外壳，除去污物在清水中冲洗干净备用。

②将肉蟹放入盘中，加葱、姜、料酒、盐、味精，上笼蒸 20 分钟至蟹肉成熟后取出，捡去葱、姜，装盘。

③旺火热锅，放入油烧至八成热后，浇在肉蟹上即可。

特点：色泽鲜红，肉质洁白细嫩

口味：原汁原味成鲜

Crab with Scallions and Ginger

Ingredients：
600 grams (1.32lb) crabs
5 grams (0.18oz) scallions cut into sections
5 grams (0.18oz) sliced ginger
25 grams (5tsp) cooking wine
6 grams (1tsp) salt
1 gram (1/4tsp) MSG
25 grams (2tbsp) cooking oil

Directions：
(1) Remove the shells and wash the crabs clean.

(2) Put the crabs on a plate, add in the scallions, ginger, cooking wine, salt and MSG and steam for 20 minutes. Pick out the scallions and ginger. Arrange the steamed crabs on a plate.

(3) Heat the oil until it is 200-220℃ (390-430℉) and sprinkle on the steamed crabs.

Features：Bright red in color on the outside but the meat is pure white and tender.

Taste：Very fresh.

葱姜肉蟹
Crab with Scallions and Ginger

清炒虾仁

主料：虾仁 350 克。

调料：鸡蛋清 1 只、盐 4 克、料酒 5 克、味精 1 克、淀粉 10 克、油 50 克、麻油 5 克、清汤 10 克，湿淀粉 10 克。

制作：①先将虾仁洗净滤干水份，加盐 4 克，鸡蛋清、淀粉，上浆备用。

②旺火热锅，加油，待油温升至四成热时，投入虾仁，溜炒至断生，倒出滤油。

③锅中留油 10 克，加料酒，清汤，味精，倒入虾仁翻炒，用湿淀粉勾芡，淋麻油出锅，装盘即成。

特点：色泽洁白

口味：鲜嫩爽滑

Stir-fried Shrimps

Ingredients：
350 grams (0.77lb) shrimps
1 egg white
4 grams (2/3tsp) salt
5 grams (1tsp) cooking wine
1 gram (1/4tsp) MSG
10 grams (1.5tbsp) dry cornstarch
50 grams (4tbsp) cooking oil
5 grams (1tsp) sesame oil
10 grams (2tsp) water
10 grams (1.5tsp) mixture of cornstarch and water

Directions：
(1) Wash the shrimps clean and drain off the water. Marinate in 4 grams (2/3tsp) of salt, one egg white and dry cornstarch.

(2) Heat the oil until it is 70-100℃ (160-210℉). Put in the shrimps in the wok and, as soon as they are no longer raw, bring them out and drain off the oil.

(3) Keep 10 grams (2tsp) of oil in the wok. Add in the cooking wine, water, MSG and shrimp. Stir-fry and then add in the cornstarch-water mixture. Sprinkle on sesame oil and put on a plate to serve.

Features：Crystal white in color.
Taste：Tender and slippery.

清炒虾仁
Stir-fried Shrimps

香炸虾球

主料：虾仁 350 克。

辅料：鸡蛋清 1 只。

调料：料酒 5 克、味精 1 克、淀粉 10 克、油 250 克（实耗 100 克），盐 4 克。

制作：①将虾仁洗净，滤干水份，再放盐 3 克，鸡蛋清半只，淀粉 10 克，上浆备用。

②将上过浆的虾仁剁成茸状，放在碗里，加料酒、味精和半只鸡蛋清搅拌上劲（用力向一个方向搅拌虾茸）后用手捏成直径 25 毫米大的丸子待用。

③旺火热锅、放油，待油温升至五成热时，用中火，放入虾球炸至金黄色，捞出装盘。

特点：色泽金黄

口味：外脆里嫩

Fried Shrimp Balls

Ingredients:
350 grams (0.77lb)shrimps
1 egg white
5 grams (1tsp)cooking wine
1 gram (1/4tsp)MSG
10 grams (1.5tbsp)dry cornstarch
250 grams (1 cup)cooking oil (only 100 grams or 8tbsp to be actually consumed)
4 grams (2/3tsp)salt

Directions:
(1)Take off the shells of the shrimps, wash clean and drain off the water. Add 3 grams (1/2tsp)of salt, half the egg white and 10 grams (1.5tbsp)of dry cornstarch and mix.

(2)Chop the shrimps into a paste and place in a bowl. Add the cooking wine, MSG and the other half of the egg white. Blend them hard in one direction. Then use your fingers to shape the shrimp paste into balls.

(3)Heat the cooking oil on a hot fire until it is 110-135°C (230-275°F) and now turn down the fire to a medium level. Place the shrimp balls in the wok to deep-fry until they are golden brown in color. Now place on a plate and serve.

Features: Golden brown in color.
Taste: Crispy outside and tender inside.

香炸虾球
Fried Shrimp Balls

滑炒鱼片

主料：草鱼鱼片 300 克。

辅料：胡萝卜 25 克、青椒 1 只切片。

调料：盐 4 克、味精 1 克、清汤 100 克、湿淀粉 15 克、淀粉 10 克、油 250 克（实耗 50 克）、料酒 10 克、鸡蛋清 1 只。

制作：①把剔去骨刺，不带皮的鱼肉切成厚约 0.3 厘米，长 5 厘米，宽 4 厘米左右的片。

②将鸡蛋清、盐、淀粉同鱼片一起搅拌上浆备用。

③旺火热锅，放油，待油温升至四成热时，倒入鱼片滑炒至熟，倒出滤油。锅留余油 5 克，投入胡萝卜、青椒片，加料酒，清汤，味精调好口味，用湿淀粉勾芡，倒入鱼片翻炒均匀，淋麻油出锅装盘，即可。

特点：鱼肉色泽洁白

口味：鲜嫩爽滑

Fried Fish Slices with Sauce

Ingredients：
300 grams (0.66lb) freshwater fish (preferably grass carp)
25 grams (0.9oz carrots sliced
1 green pepper sliced
4 grams (2/3tsp) salt
1 gram (1/4tsp) MSG
100 grams (6tbsp) water
15 grams (1.5tbsp) mixture of cornstarch and water
10 grams (1.5tbsp) dry cornstarch
250 grams (1 cup) cooking oil (only 50 grams or 4tbsp to be actually consumed)
10 grams (2tsp) cooking wine
1 egg white

Directions：
(1) Cut the boneless and skinless fish into slices of about 0.3 cm (0.12 in) in thickness, 5 cm (2 in) long and 4 cm (1.6in) wide.

(2) Mix the egg white, salt and dry cornstarch with the fish slices.

(3) Heat the cooking oil over a hot fire until it is 70-100℃ (160-210°F). Throw in the fish slices and let them fry until they are done. Remove the oil but keep 5 grams (1tsp) in the wok. Put in the carrot and green pepper slices, add the cooking wine, water and MSG. Thicken the sauce by adding the cornstarch-water mixture. Put in the already fried fish slices and stir. Sprinkle sesame oil and place on a plate ready for eating.

Features：The fish meat is pure white and shiny.
Taste：Refreshing and smooth.

滑炒鱼片
Fried Fish Slices with Sauce

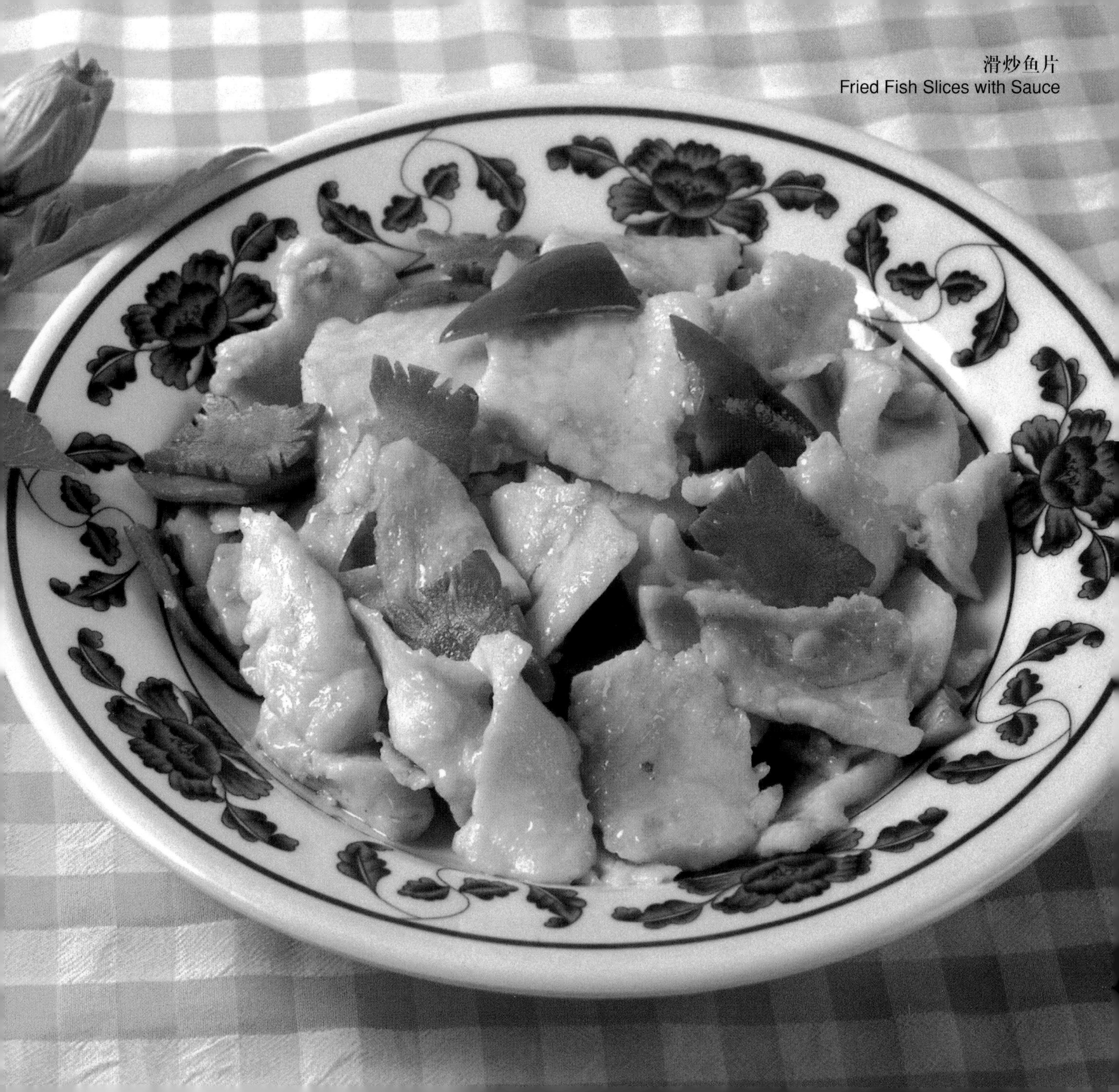

翡翠虾仁

主料：虾仁 300 克。

辅料：青椒 10 只、熟火腿末 5 克。

调料：清汤 50 克、料酒 15 克、盐 6 克、糖 3 克、味精 2 克、湿淀粉 15 克、淀粉 20 克、油 250 克（实耗 100 克）、鸡蛋清 1 只。

制作：①虾仁洗净，滤干水份放盐 4 克、鸡蛋清、淀粉上浆备用。

②青椒选灯笼形，去蒂籽，洗净用刀在蒂口周围刻成花瓣型，滤干水。

③将炒锅置中火烧热，倒入油烧至四成热时，倒入青椒炸至呈翠绿色，倒出油后，锅中加水 150 克，味精 1 克，盐 2 克，翻烧 1 分钟，倒出青椒滤干水份，口朝上，排在盘中备用。

④锅置火上，放油 25 克，油热至五成，倒入虾仁翻炒，放清汤、料酒、味精 1 克调好口味，放入湿淀粉勾芡，翻炒，淋麻油起锅，装入青椒中，撒上火腿末即成。

特点：绿白相间，造型美观。

口味：鲜美滑嫩

Shrimps with Green Peppers

Ingredients：
300 grams (0.66lb) shrimps
10 green peppers
5 grams (0.18oz) cooked ham, minced
50 grams (3tbsp) water
15 grams (3tsp) cooking wine
6 grams (1tsp) salt
3 grams (2/3tsp) sugar
2 grams (1/2tsp) MSG
15 grams (1tbsp) mixture of cornstarch and water
20 grams (4tbsp) dry cornstarch
250 grams (1 cup) cooking oil (only 100 grams or 8tbsp to be actually consumed)
1 egg white

Directions：
(1) Wash the shrimps clean, drain them and mix with 4 grams (2/3tsp) of salt, the egg white and dry cornstarch.

(2) Select the lantern-shaped green peppers, remove their stems and seeds, wash them clean, and cut petal-shaped patterns around where the stems used to be.

(3) Heat the cooking oil until it is about 70-100℃ (160-210℉). Put in the green peppers and cook until they turn bright green. Pour out the oil, add 150 grams (10tbsp) of water, 1 gram (1/4tsp) of MSG and 2 grams (1/3tsp) of salt to stir-fry for one minute. Take out the green peppers and place them on a plate, keeping their opening in view.

(4) Put 25 grams (2tbsp) of oil in the wok and heat until it is about 110-135℃ (230-275℉). Put in the shrimps and stir-fry, Add the water, cooking wine, and 1 gram (1/4tsp) of MSG and pour in the cornstarch-water mixture to thicken the sauce. Keep stir-frying. Sprinkle in a few drops of sesame oil and put the green peppers into the wok. Spread the minced ham on the shrimps and green peppers and the dish is ready to serve.

Features：The white and green colors as well as the shapes of the green peppers and shrimps form nice combinations.
Taste：Refreshing and succulent.

翡翠虾仁
Shrimps with Green Peppers

番茄汁虾球

主料：虾仁 350 克。

辅料：火腿 50 克。

调料：鸡蛋清 2 只、料酒 5 克、糖 5 克、味精 1 克、湿淀粉 20 克、番茄酱 100 克、清汤 50 克、盐 3 克、油 250 克（实耗 100 克）、淀粉 10 克。

制作：①虾仁洗净，滤干水份，加鸡蛋清 1 只，盐 3 克，淀粉 10 克，上浆备用，火腿切成末。

②将浆好的虾仁剁成细茸放在碗里，加料酒 3 克，鸡蛋清 1 只，火腿末搅拌上劲（用力顺一个方面搅拌），然后用手捏成直径约 2 厘米大小的丸子待用。

③旺火热锅放油，待油温升至六成热时，放入丸子改中火炸至金黄色成熟后，捞出滤油。

④锅内留余油 10 克，加热后，加入清汤、料酒 2 克、糖、番茄酱、味精、虾丸，翻炒至卤汁收浓后，用湿淀粉勾芡，翻炒，淋麻油出锅，装盘即成。

特点：色泽鲜红

口味：酸甜可口

Shrimp Balls in Tomato Sauce

Ingredients：

350 grams (0.77lb)shrimps
50 grams (0.11lb)ham
2 egg whites
5 grams (1tsp)cooking wine
5 grams (1tsp)sugar
1 gram (1/4tsp)MSG
20 grams (1.5tbsp)mixture of cornstarch and water
100 grams (5.5tbsp)tomato sauce
50 grams (3tbsp)water
3 grams (1/2tsp)salt
250 grams (1 cup)cooking oil (only 100 grams or 8tbsp to be actually consumed)
10 grams (1.5tbsp)dry cornstarch

Directions：

(1)Wash the shrimps clean and drain off the water. Mix the shrimps with 1 egg white, 3 grams (1/2tsp) of salt and 10 grams (1.5tbsp)of dry cornstarch. Chop the ham into mince.

(2) Chop the shrimps into fine mince and place into a bowl. Add 3 grams (3/5tsp)of cooking wine, 1 egg white and the minced ham and stir in one direction. Then shape the mixture into balls of 2 cm (0.8in)in diameter with fingers.

(3)Heat the oil until it is about 135-170℃ (275-340°F). Place the shrimp balls into the hot oil to deep-fry until they are golden yellow in color. Take them out and drain off the oil.

(4)Leave 10 grams (2tsp)of oil in the wok, add the water, tomato sauce, 2 grams (2tsp) of cooking wine, sugar, MSG, and shrimp balls to stir-fry. Add the cornstarch-water mixture to thicken the gravy, continue to stir-fry. Sprinkle sesame oil and place the shrimp balls onto a plate to serve.

Features：Bright red in color.
Taste：Sweet and sour in taste.

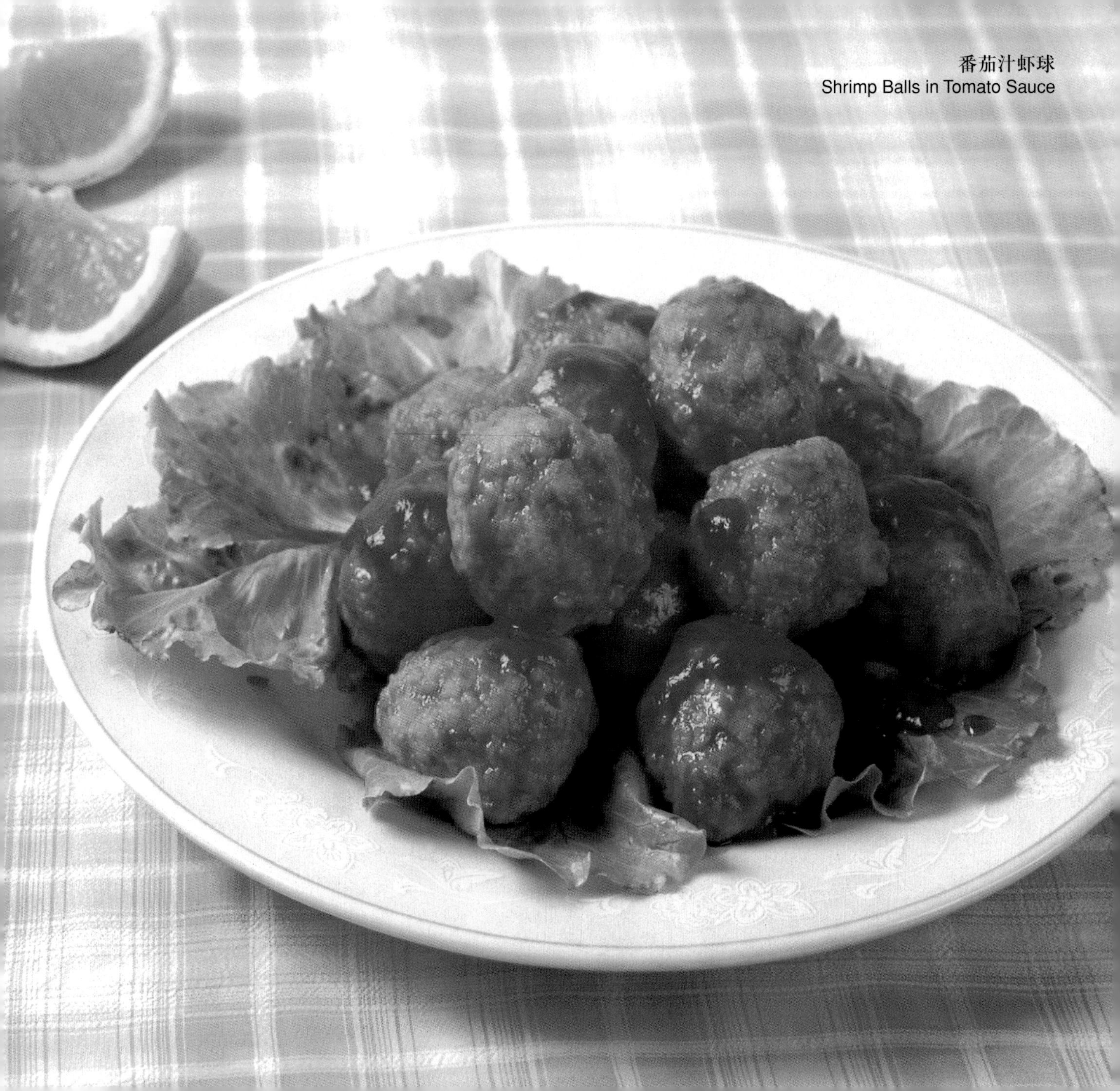

番茄汁虾球
Shrimp Balls in Tomato Sauce

糖醋鱼

主料：黄鱼 1 条（约 750 克）。

调料：番茄酱 150 克、油 500 克（实耗 100 克）、白醋 50 克、糖 150 克、盐 6 克、蒜茸 2 克、味精 2 克、清汤 100 克、淀粉 150 克、湿淀粉 50 克、料酒 25 克。

制作：①鱼杀洗干净、用刀在鱼身上正反两面各平行划 4 刀，然后用盐 4 克和料酒腌渍 15 分钟。

②在腌渍后的鱼的两面拍上淀粉，抖去余粉备用。

③旺火热锅，放油，待油温升至七成热时，把鱼投入油锅炸至金黄色后，倒出滤油，装入盘中。

④锅内留余油 10 克，加热后，放入蒜茸炒出香味，再放番茄酱、盐 2 克、味精、清汤、白醋调好口味，倒入湿淀粉勾芡，出锅浇在炸好的鱼身上即可。

特点：色泽金红色，造型美观

口味：外脆里嫩，鱼肉鲜香，卤汁甜酸可口

Sweet and Sour Fish

Ingredients：

1 seawater fish（yellow croaker）（about 750 grams or 1.65lb)

150 grams (8tbsp)tomato sauce

500 grams (2 cups)cooking oil (only 100 grams or 8tbsp to be actually consumed)

50 grams (3tbsp)white vinegar

150 (11.5tbsp)grams sugar

6 grams (1tsp)salt

2 grams (0.07oz)minced garlic

2 grams (1/2tsp)MSG

100 grams (6tbsp)water

150 grams (3/4 cup)dry cornstarch

50 grams (2.7tbsp)mixture of cornstarch and water

25 grams (5tsp)cooking wine

Directions：

(1) Clean the fish and on each side make four horizontal cuts. Marinate the fish with 4 grams (2/3tsp)of salt and the cooking wine.

(2)Dust the fish with dry cornstarch on both sides and then shake off the unnecessary cornstarch that does not stick to the fish.

(3) Heat the oil until about 180-200℃ (355-390°F). Put in the fish to deep-fry and then take it out when it is golden brown in color.

(4) Leave 10 grams (2tsp) of oil in the wok and fry the minced garlic until it releases its aromatic smell. Add the tomato sauce, sugar, 2 grams (1/3tsp)of salt, MSG, water and vinegar. Put in the cornstarch-water mixture to thicken the sauce. Now place the fish on a plate to serve.

Features：Golden in color and beautiful in shape.

Taste：Crispy outside and tender inside. The fish is refreshingly tasty and the sauce is invitingly sweet and sour.

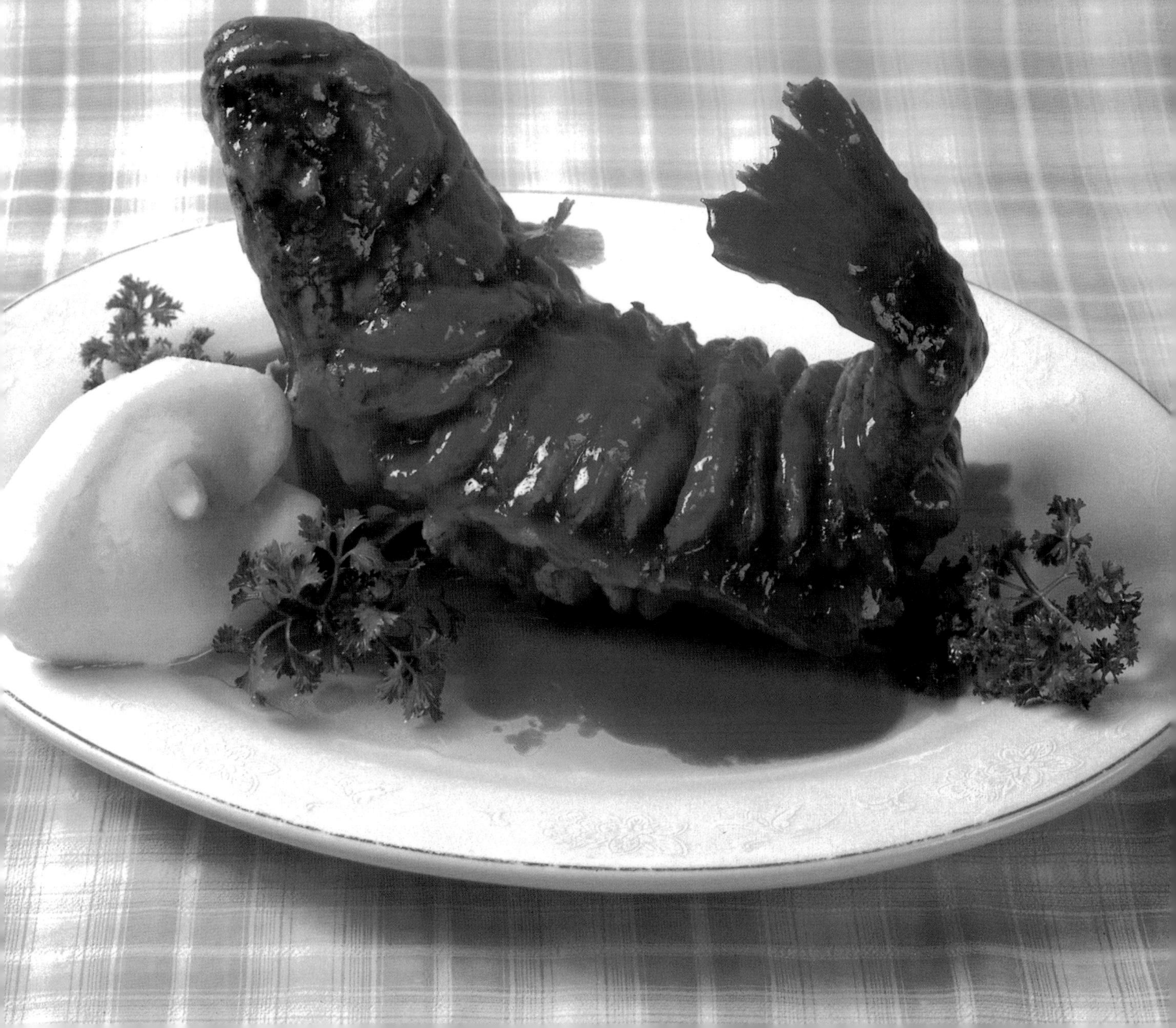

糖醋鱼
Sweet and Sour Fish

松鼠鱼

主料：鳜鱼 1 条（约 750 克）。

辅料：虾仁 30 克、笋丁 20 克、水发香菇丁 20 克, 青豌豆 15 粒（左右）。

调料：料酒 20 克、盐 7 克、糖 150 克、香醋 100 克、番茄酱 100 克、淀粉 500 克（实耗 100 克左右）、清汤 100 克、湿淀粉 35 克、麻油 10 克、油 1000 克（实耗 200 克）。

制作：①鱼洗杀干净，把鱼平放在砧板上，用刀沿胸鳍切下鱼头，从头颈部用刀沿鱼脊背骨两侧剖切至鱼尾（不切断鱼尾），斩去鱼背骨，再用刀沿肋骨侧线平行割去胸刺骨，在两片鱼肉内侧，先纵向直刀，刀距 1 厘米，再横向划，刀距 2 厘米，纵横刀深均至皮（不能破皮），成菱形小块，用料酒 10 克、盐 5 克，腌渍 5 分钟，然后在鱼头、鱼肉上拍上淀粉，用手捏住鱼尾,抖去余粉,备用。

②旺火热锅放油，待油温升至八成热时，把刚拍好粉的鱼向内翻卷，鱼皮在里，鱼肉在外，一手持鱼尾，一手用筷子夹住另一端，放入油锅中炸，待成形后松手，放入鱼头同炸至熟，捞出，装在盘中，安上鱼头。

③另取容器放番茄酱、清汤、糖，料酒 10 克，盐 2 克，合成卤汁备用。

④锅中留余油 20 克，放入虾仁，笋丁，水发香菇丁，青豌豆，翻炒至熟后，倒入卤汁，烧沸后用湿淀粉勾芡，淋热麻油出锅，浇在炸好的鳜鱼身上即成。

特点：造型美观，形似松鼠

口味：酸甜可口，外脆里嫩

Sweet and Sour Fish in Squirrel Shape

Ingredients：

1 freshwater fish (preferably manderin fish)of about 750 grams (1.65lb)

30grams (1.1oz)shrimps

20grams (0.7oz)diced bamboo shoots

20grams (0.7oz)diced mushrooms (originally dried mushrooms that have been soaked in water) 15 grams (0.53oz)green peas

20grams (4tsp)cooking wine

7 grams (1.1tsp)salt

150grams (11.5tbsp)sugar

100grams (6.5tbsp) vinegar

100grams (5.5tbsp)tomato sauce

500grams (1.1lb) dry cornstarch (only about 100 grams or 0.22lb to be actually used)

100grams (6tbsp)water

35grams (2tbsp)mixture of cornstarch and water

10grams (2tsp)sesame oil

1000grams (4cups) cooking oil (200grams or 4/5cup to be actually consumed)

Directions：

(1)Clean the fish, cut off the head near the belly fin, but do not throw it away. Cut open the fish along its back until the cut reaches its tail. (Do not cut off the tail.)Cut out the back bone and remove the side bones (ribs). Make several cuts with 1 cm spaces in between, first vertically and then horizontally on the inner side of the fish to create a diamond-shaped pattern. (Do not cut open the skin.)Marinate the fish with 10grams (2tsp)of cooking wine and 5grams (5/6tsp)of salt for 5minutes. Dust the dry cornstarch on the fish body and head. Hold the fish tail to shake off unnecessary cornstarch.

(2)Heat the oil until it is about 200-220℃ (390-430℉). Roll the fish to keep the skin inside. Hold the fish tail with one hand and the top end of the fish body with chopsticks and gradually release it into the oil. Now place the head into the oil also. When both are done, take them out and place them on a plate, putting the head and the body together to create the concept of a whole fish.

(3) Mix the tomato sauce, water, sugar, 10 grams (2tsp) of cooking wine and 2grams (1/3tsp)of salt into a sauce.

(4) Keep 20grams (1.5tbsp) of oil in the wok. Put in the shrimps, diced bamboo shoots, mushrooms and green peas and stir-fry. Add in the mixed sauce. When the sauce is boiling, put in the cornstarch-water mixture to thicken it. Sprinkle some sesame oil and pour the sauce right onto the fish.

Features：It beautifully resembles the shape of a squirrel.

Taste：Both sweet and sour, crispy outside and tender inside.

松鼠鱼
Sweet and Sour Fish in Squirrel Shape

红烧鱼段

主料：带鱼 400 克。

辅料：笋片 25 克。

调料：料酒 25 克、酱油 20 克、糖 10 克、味精 1 克、油 50 克、葱段、姜片各 5 克、清汤 200 克。

制作：①将鱼洗杀干净，切成 8 厘米长的段，放入盘中，加酱油少许，腌渍 5 分钟。

②旺火烧锅，放油，待油温升六成热时，把鱼逐段放入，煎至酱红色时捞出。

③旺火加热锅中余油，放入葱、姜煸出香味，放入煎好的鱼段、笋片，加入料酒，加盖加闷，加入酱油、糖、清汤，加锅盖烧七八分钟至鱼肉熟，卤汁稠浓时，加味精，出锅装盘即成。

特点：色泽红亮

口味：咸鲜中略有甜味

Braised Fish Sections

Ingredients：
400 grams (0.88lb) seawater fish (hairtail)
25 grams (0.9oz) sliced bamboo shoots
25 grams (5tsp) cooking wine
20 grams (1tbsp) soy sauce
10 grams (2tsp) sugar
1 gram (1/4tsp) MSG
50 grams (4tbsp) cooking oil
5 grams (0.18oz) sectioned scallions
5 grams (0.18oz) ginger slices
200 grams (4/5 cup) water

Directions：
(1) Clean the fish, cut into sections of 8 cm (about 3 in) long, place in a dish, add some soy sauce and let marinate for 5 minutes.

(2) Heat the wok, add oil and heat it until temperature reaches 135-170℃ (275-340℉). Place the fish sections into the oil to fry until brown.

(3) Put the scallions and ginger slices into the remaining oil until they give out fragrance. Add the deep-fried fish sections, bamboo shoot slices and cooking wine. Cover up the wok and let simmer. Add the soy sauce, sugar, water and simmer again for 7 to 8 minutes until the fish meat is well done and the sauce is thick. Add the MSG and place the fish in a serving dish.

Features：Bright red in color.
Taste：It has a slight sweet quality.

红烧鱼段
Braised Fish Sections

果汁鱼块

主料：草鱼肉 300 克。

调料：果汁芡 75 克（果汁芡是番茄酱 20 克，果汁 20 克，清汤 30 克，糖 4 克、盐 1 克混合烧沸而成）、鸡蛋 1 只、盐 2 克、淀粉 30 克、湿淀粉 10 克、油 250 克（实耗 50 克）料酒 10 克。

制作：①将鱼杀好，洗净，切成 2 厘米厚的小块，鱼块同盐、料酒一起腌渍 10 分钟后，打入鸡蛋，湿淀粉拌匀，捞出拍上淀粉备用。

②旺火热锅，放油，待油温升至 6 成热时，放入鱼块，炸至金黄色捞出装盘。

③锅内留余油 15 克加热倒入果汁芡及炸过的鱼块翻炒后淋油出锅装盘。

特点：色泽鲜红

口味：甜中带酸

Fish in Fruit Sauce

Ingredients:

300 grams (0.66lb) freshwater grass carp meat

75 grams (5tbsp) fruit sauce (made of 20 grams or1tbsp of tomato sauce, 20 grams or 1.5tbsp of fruit juice, 30 grams or 2tbsp of water, 4 grams or 1tsp of sugar and 1 gram or 1/6tsp of salt cooked together to boiling point)

1 egg

2 grams (1/3tsp) salt

30 grams (5tbsp) dry cornstarch

10 grams (1.5tsp) mixture of cornstarch and water

250 grams (1 cup) cooking oil (only 50 grams or 4tbsp to be consumed)

10 grams (2tsp) cooking wine

Directions:

(1) Clean the fish and cut into dices 2 cm (0.8in) on each side. Marinate in salt and cooking wine for 10 minutes. Then add the egg and cornstarch-water mixture and stir. Dust with dry cornstarch and put aside.

(2) Heat the wok over a hot fire, add oil and heat until 135-170℃ (275-340°F). Put in the fish dices and until brown. Remove and place on a dish.

(3) Pour out all but 15 grams (1tbsp) of oil. Heat it and add the fruit sauce and fish dices. Stir, sprinkle sesame oil and put on the serving dish.

Features: Bright red in color.

Taste: Sweet with a slight sour taste.

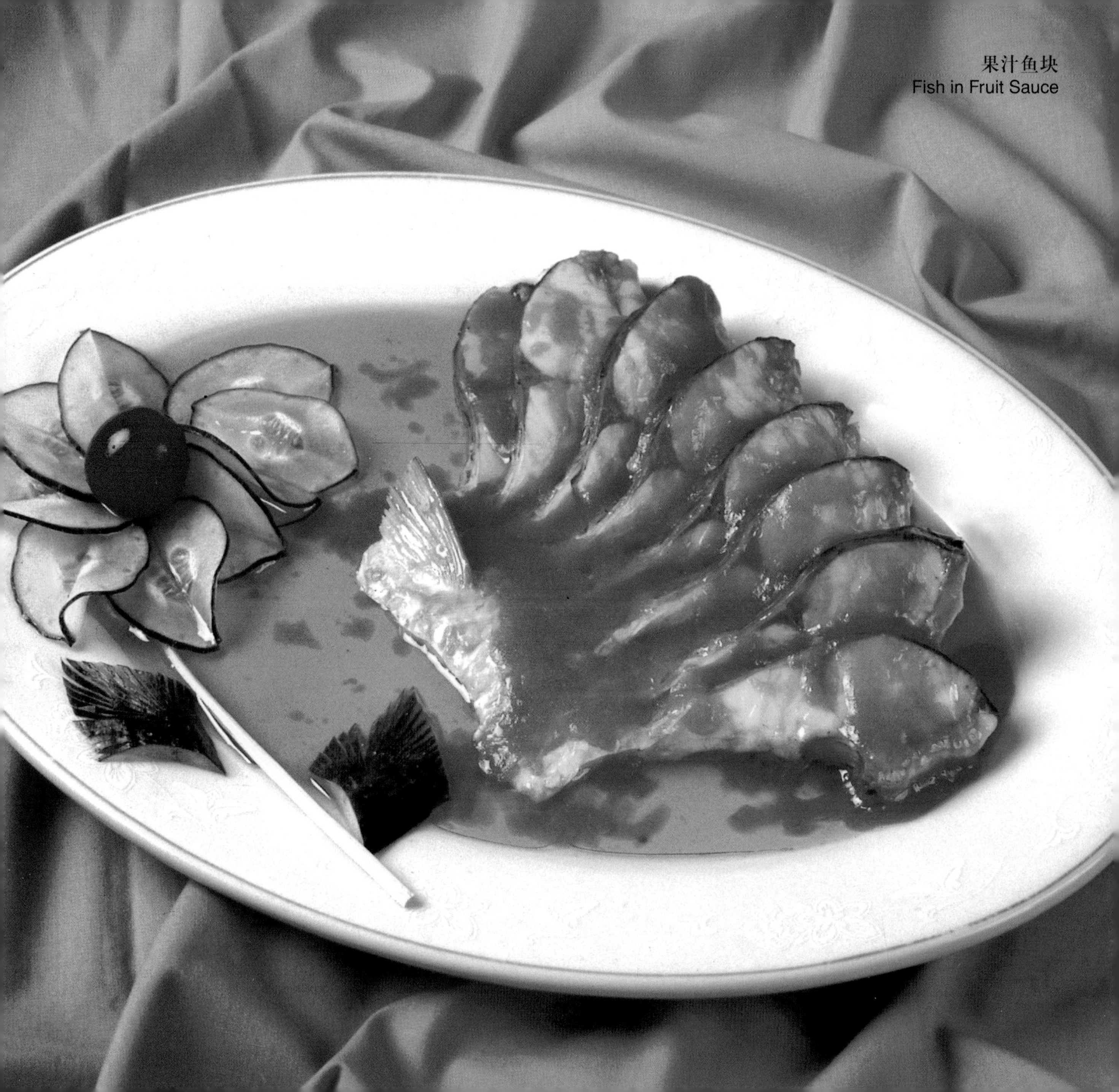

果汁鱼块
Fish in Fruit Sauce

红烧肉蟹

主料：肉蟹 600 克。

调料：料酒 20 克、酱油 10 克、糖 5 克、盐 4 克、葱、姜末各 5 克、油 50 克、面粉 25 克、味精 1 克、清汤 200 克。

制作：①将肉蟹剥去背壳去除污物，冲洗干净，每只一切两块，蟹钳和腿用刀背拍碎（以便烧时入味）。

②旺火烧锅倒入油，放入葱、姜煸炒出香味，再放下肉蟹炒至蟹壳变红，约 2 分钟。放料酒加盖焖二分钟后，再放酱油、盐、糖、清汤，烧 10 分钟左右至卤汁浓稠时，将面粉加清水拌和成的厚浆倒入锅中炒和，加入味精，淋油出锅，装盘即成。

特点：色泽深红油亮
口味：肉嫩味美

Braised Crabs

Ingredients：
600 grams (1.32lb) crabs
20 grams (4tsp) cooking wine
10 grams (1.5tsp) soy sauce
5 grams (1tsp) sugar
4 grams (2/3tsp) salt
5 grams (0.18oz) chopped scallions
5 grams (0.18oz) finely chopped ginger
50 grams (1tsp) cooking oil
25 grams (4tbsp) wheat flour
1 gram (1/4tsp) MSG
200 grams (4/5 cup) water

Directions：
(1) Remove the shells and wash the crabs clean. Cut each in two halves and, for easy absorption of the sauce, crush the pincers and legs with the dull edge of the cooking chopper.

(2) Use hot fire to heat oil in the wok. Put in the scallions and ginger until they give forth their aroma. Now put in the crabs and stir-fry until they turn red, usually in about 2 minutes. Add the cooking wine and simmer for 2 minutes. Add the soy sauce, salt, sugar and water and cook for 10 minutes until the sauce turns thick. Mix the flour with water to turn it into paste. Put this in the wok and stir. Add the MSG, sprinkle sesame oil and the dish is ready to eat.

Features：Dark red and shiny in color.
Taste：Tender and delicious.

红烧肉蟹
Braised Crabs

蚝油鱼球

主料：草鱼鱼肉 300 克。

调料：淀粉 10 克、蚝油 30 克、酱油 5 克、糖和盐各 3 克、味精 1 克、清汤 50 克、油 100 克（实耗 50 克）、鸡蛋清 1 只、湿淀粉 25 克。

制作：①把除去头、尾、骨、刺和皮的鱼肉用刀切成小块，放鸡蛋清、淀粉、盐 2 克上浆备用。

②15 分钟后，将上过浆的鱼肉，剁成鱼茸，加料酒上劲（用力朝一个方向搅拌）用手捏成直径约 2 厘米的丸子备用。

③旺火烧锅放油，待油温升至六成热时，转小火，将丸子分批投入炸至呈金黄色捞出。

④原锅留余油 10 克，加蚝油、酱油、糖、盐 1 克，味精、清汤烧开后倒入炸好的丸子翻炒 1 分钟左右，用湿淀粉勾芡，淋油出锅，装盘即成。

特点：色泽油亮

口味：鲜香入味

Fish Balls in Oyster Sauce

Ingredients：

300 grams (0.66lb) freshwater grass carp meat

10 grams (1.5tbsp) dry cornstarch

30 grams (1.6tbsp) oyster sauce

5 grams (1tsp) soy sauce

3 grams (1/2tsp) of salt

3 grams (2/3tsp) of sugar

1 gram (1/4tsp) MSG

50 grams (3tbsp) water

100 grams (8tbsp) cooking oil (only 50 grams or 4tbsp to be actually consumed)

1 egg white

25 grams (1.5tbsp) mixture of cornstarch and water

Directions：

(1) Cut the headless, tailless, boneless and skinless fish into small dices. Add the egg white, cornstarch and salt to the fish dices and marinate for 15 minutes.

(2) Chop the marinated fish into mince meat, add the cooking wine and stir quickly in one direction. Make the minced meat into balls of 2 cm (0.8in) in diameter with fingers.

(3) Heat the oil with a hot fire to 135-170℃ (275-340℉). Turn the fire down and deepfry the meat balls to brown in color. Remove from the wok.

(4) Keep 10 grams (2tsp) of cooking oil in the wok. Add the oyster sauce, soy sauce, sugar, 1 gram (1/6tsp) of salt, MSG and water. At boiling point, put in the deep-fried fish meat balls and stir for 1 minute. Add the cornstarch-water mixture to thicken the sauce. Sprinkle sesame oil and place the fish balls on a plate.

Features：Shiny.

Taste：Richly delicious.

蚝油鱼球
Fish Balls in Oyster Sauce

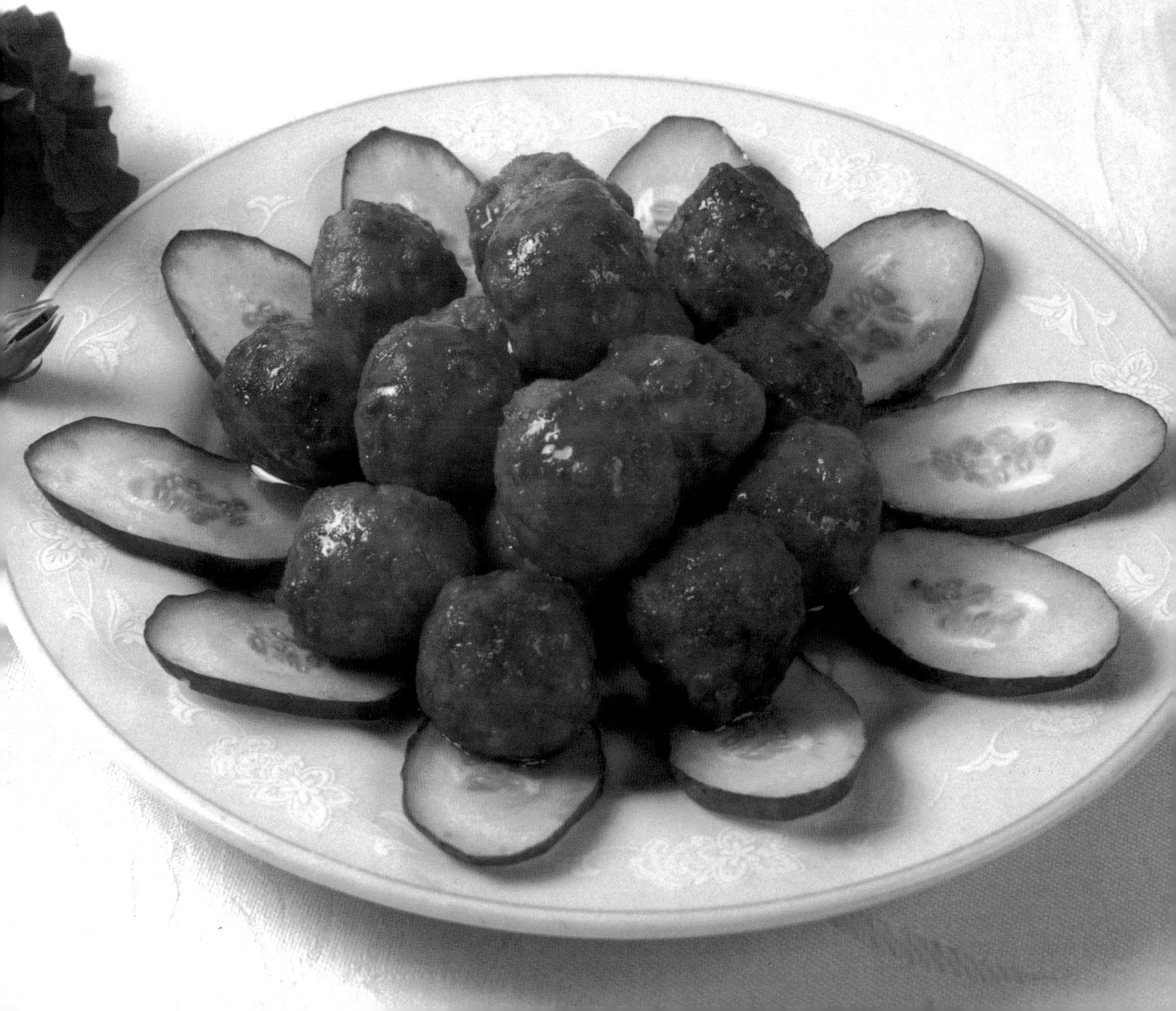

龙井虾仁

主料：虾仁 350 克。

辅料：龙井新茶（或其它绿茶）1 克。

调料：料酒 5 克、味精 1 克、盐 3 克、淀粉 10 克、鸡蛋清 1 只、油 50 克。

制作：①虾仁洗净，滤干水份，加盐 2 克，鸡蛋清，淀粉上浆备用。

②取茶杯 1 只，放入茶叶，用沸水 150 克泡开，放 1 分钟后滤去茶汁，剩下茶叶备用。

③旺火烧锅放油，待油温升至五成热时，放入虾仁，溜炒断生，放入茶叶，放入料酒，盐 1 克，味精，大火翻炒，淋油出锅装盘。

特点：色泽洁白，带有少许翠绿色

口味：鲜嫩味美，茶香扑鼻

Dragon Well Shrimps

Ingredients：
350 grams（0.77lb）shrimps
1 gram（1tsp）Dragon Well Tea（or other green tea）（picked most recently）
5 grams（1tsp）cooking wine
1 gram（1/4tsp）MSG
3 grams（1/2tsp）salt
10 grams（1.5tbsp）dry cornstarch
1 egg white
50 grams（4tbsp）cooking oil

Directions：
（1）Wash the shrimps clean, drain off the water, add 2 grams（1/3tsp）of salt, the egg white and cornstarch, and let marinate.

（2）Put the tea in a teacup, add 150 grams（3/5 cup）of boiling water and let the water stay for 1 minute. Pour out the water and keep the tea leaves for use later.

（3）Heat the oil with a hot fire until about 110-135℃（230-275℉）. Put in the shrimps and quickly stir-fry. Add the tea leaves, cooking wine, 1 gram（1/6tsp）f salt and MSG. Stir-fry. Sprinkle on sesame oil and put the dish on a plate to serve.

Features：White-colored shrimps dotted with fresh green tea leaves.

Taste：Refreshing and aromatic.

龙井虾仁
Dragon Well Shrimps

鱼炖蛋

主料： 鲫鱼1条（约250克）。

辅料： 鸡蛋3只。

调料： 油2克、盐3克、味精1克、清汤150克、葱姜汁5克（葱、姜末用水泡片刻，去渣即成）、料酒5克。

制作： ①鱼去鳞、鳃、内脏，洗干净，锅内放清水1000克，旺火烧沸后，放入鱼焯1分钟捞出，用清水冲洗干净放入器皿中备用。

②鸡蛋打入碗内打散后，加盐、味精、清汤、料酒、油、姜葱汁、搅拌均匀后，倒入焯过的鱼中，上笼蒸10分钟即可。

特点： 色泽淡黄

口味： 鱼肉细嫩，鸡蛋味鲜

Fish in Egg Custard

Ingredients：

1 freshwater fish (crucian carp)of about 250 grams (0.55lb)
3 eggs
2 grams (1/2tsp)cooking oil
3 grams (1/2tsp)salt
1 gram (1/4tsp)MSG
150 grams (3/5 cup)water
5 grams (1tsp)scallion and ginger juice (Soak finely chopped ginger and scallions in water and then remove them from the water)
5 grams (1tsp)cooking wine

Directions：

(1) Gut the fish, remove its scales and fins and wash it clean. Put 1,000 grams (4 cups)of water in a pot over hot fire. When it boils, put the fish in the water for 1 minute. Take it out, wash it again and put into a container.

(2) Break and beat the eggs. Add the salt, MSG, water, cooking wine, oil, and ginger and scallion juice. Stir this well. Put the fish onto the egg mixture and steam for 10 minutes.

Features： Light yellow in color.

Taste： The fish meat is tender and the eggs taste delicious.

鱼炖蛋
Fish in Egg Custard

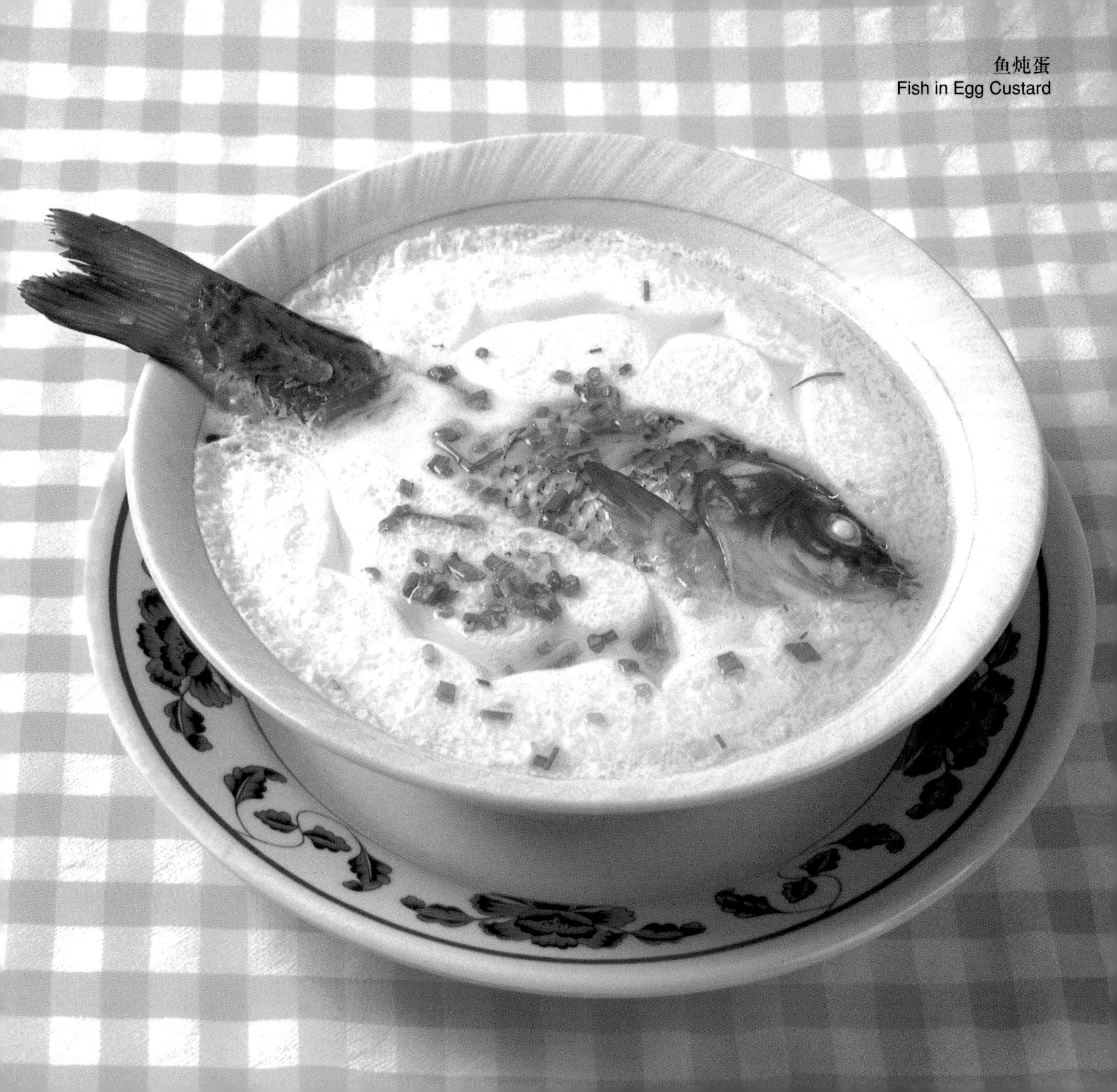

瓜姜鱼丝

主料：草鱼鱼肉 300 克。

辅料：罐装甜酱瓜丝 8 克、罐装嫩酱姜丝 8 克。

调料：鸡蛋清 1 只、料酒 10 克、盐 2 克、味精 1 克、湿淀粉 10 克、油 70 克、清汤 50 克、淀粉 5 克。

制作：①将去骨、刺、皮的净鱼肉 300 克，洗净滤干水份，切成长 7 厘米，宽、厚各 0.4 厘米的丝，再放盐 2 克，鸡蛋清 1 只，淀粉 5 克，拌匀后，上浆备用。

②旺火烧锅，放油 50 克，待油温升至五成热时，放下鱼丝滑炒至熟，倒出。锅内放油 20 克，加热后投入甜酱瓜丝，嫩酱姜丝，料酒，味精，清汤，调好口味，放入湿淀粉勾芡，倒入鱼丝翻炒，淋油，出锅，装盘。

特点：鱼肉洁白。

口味：鲜嫩香脆，咸鲜适口

Quick-fried Fish Shreds with Cucumbers and Ginger in Soy Sauce

Ingredients：

300 grams (0.66lb) freshwater fish (grass carp) fillets
8 grams (0.3oz) canned pickled cucumber shreds
8 grams (0.3oz) canned pickled ginger shreds
1 egg
10 grams (2tsp) cooking wine
2 grams (1/3tsp) salt
1 gram (1/4tsp) MSG
10 grams (1.5tsp) mixture of cornstarch and water
70 grams (5tbsp) of cooking oil
50 grams (3tbsp) of water
5 grams (1tbsp) of dry cornstarch

Directions：

(1) Take 300 grams (0.66lb) fish meat without bones and skin, wash clean, drain off the water and cut into shreds 7 cm (2.8in) long, 0.4 cm (0.16 in) thick and wide. Marinate in 2 grams (1/3tsp) of salt, 1 egg white and 5 grams (1tbsp) of dry cornstarch.

(2) Heat the oil over a hot fire until it is 110-135℃ (230-275℉). Put in the fish shreds and quick-fry until they are done. Remove from the wok. Put 20 grams (1.5tbsp) oil in the wok, heat it, add the pickled cucumber and ginger shreds, cooking wine, MSG and water. Try the taste. Add the mixture of cornstarch and water, the fish shreds, sesame oil, stir and remove to a serving plate.

Features：The fish shreds are pure white.
Taste：Savory, aromatic and crispy.

瓜姜鱼丝
Quick-fried Fish Shreds with Cucumbers and Ginger
in Soy Sauce

清炒三虾

主料：带子河虾 1000 克

调料：鸡蛋清 1 只、料酒 25 克、盐 4 克、味精 1 克、葱姜末各 3 克、淀粉 10 克、湿淀粉 15 克、油 60 克、清汤 50 克。

制作：①将虾放入清水中洗下虾子，滤去水份，将虾子放入炒锅，加料酒 10 克，炒熟倒入盘中备用。将虾头摘下，投入沸水锅中，变硬后捞出，剥去头壳，取红色虾脑备用。虾身剥去外壳成虾仁冲洗干净，滤干水份，放盐 2 克、鸡蛋清、淀粉拌匀上浆备用。

②旺火烧锅放油 50 克，待油温升至四成热时，放入虾仁断生后，倒出。原锅加油 10 克，加葱姜末、虾子、虾脑煸炒几下后，加料酒 15 克、味精、盐 2 克、清汤，烧沸后调好味，用湿淀粉勾芡，放入虾仁翻炒均匀，淋油出锅，装盘即可。

特点：选料严格，色、香、味俱佳。

口味：鲜、美、嫩、滑

Stir-fried Shrimps

Ingredients:

1,000 grams (2.2lb) freshwater shrimps, select those with roe
1 egg white
25 grams (2tbsp) cooking wine
4 grams (2/3tsp) salt
1 gram (1/4tsp) MSG
3 grams (0.1oz) finely cut scallions
3 grams (0.1oz) finely chopped ginger
10 grams (1.5tbsp) dry cornstarch
15 grams (0.8tbsp) mixture of cornstarch and water
60 grams (4.5tbsp) cooking oil
50 grams (3tbsp) water

Directions:

(1) Wash off the shrimp roe and drain off the water. Put the shrimp roe in the wok, add 10 grams (2tsp) of cooking wine, Stir-fry and put on a dish. Take off the shrimp heads and put in to boil. Remove from water once heads become hardened. Peel off the head shell and keep the red brain for use later. Remove the shell from the body of the shrimps. The shrimps are to be washed with distilled water, the water to be drained off. Add 2 grams (1/3tsp) of salt, egg white and cornstarch.

(2) Heat 50 grams (4tbsp) of oil over a hot fire until 70-100℃ (160-210℉). Put the shrimps in and quickly remove them. Add the remaining 10 grams (2tsp) of oil to the wok. Put in the ginger, scallions, shrimp roe and shrimp brain. Quickly stir-fry. Add 15 grams (3tsp) of cooking wine, MSG, 2 grams (1/3tsp) of salt, water and let the sauce boil. Thicken it with the cornstarch-water mixture, add the shrimps, stir-fry, sprinkle the sesame oil and put the dish in a serving plate.

Features: Strictly select the raw materials for the best results in the color, aroma and taste.

Taste: Savory, delicious, tender and succulent.

清炒三虾
Stir-fried Shrimps

干烧鱼

主料：活鳜鱼 1 条约 500 克。

辅料：猪（牛）肉末 50 克、榨菜末 10 克。

调料：油 50 克、酱油 20 克、味精 1 克、料酒 20 克、糖 10 克、豆瓣酱 5 克、辣椒粉 1 克，另外，泡辣椒末、葱末、姜末、蒜末各 5 克。

制作：①鱼宰杀后，去鳞、鳃、内脏，洗干净。鱼背肉厚处，用刀剞"十"字。

②旺火烧锅放油，待油温升至七成热时，放入鱼煎至两面金黄色捞出，原锅留下煎鱼的油，放入泡辣椒末，煸出辣香味。再放豆瓣酱、辣椒粉、葱末、姜末、蒜末、榨菜末，肉末煸炒至油色变红，然后放入料酒、酱油、糖、鱼和适量的清水，旺火烧沸后，再改小火烧至熟，再开大火烧至汤汁浓稠，即可出锅装盘

特点：色泽深红，油亮

口味：辣香扑鼻

Dry-fried Fish

Ingredients：

1 live freshwater manderin fish about 500 grams (1.1lb)
50 grams (0.22lb) minced pork or beef
10 grams (0.36oz) finely chopped hot pickled mustard tubers
50 grams (4tbsp) cooking oil
20 grams (1tbsp) soy sauce
1 gram (1/4tsp) MSG
20 grams (4tsp) cooking wine
10 grams (2tsp) sugar
5 grams (1tsp) thick broad-bean sauce
1 gram (1/2tsp) hot pepper powder
5 grams (2tsp) pepper powder mixed with water
5 grams (0.18oz) finely cut scallions
5 grams (0.18oz) finely chopped ginger
5 grams (0.18oz) crushed garlic

Directions：

(1) Gut the fish, remove the scales and gills, wash the fish clean. Make cross-shaped cuts where the meat is thick.

(2) Heat the oil in the wok with a hot fire until the oil is 180-200℃ (355-390℉). Put the fish in the oil to deep-fry and remove when both sides are golden brown in color. Keep the oil in the wok and add the mixture of pepper powder and water until there is a smell of spicy fragrance. Put in the thick broad-bean sauce, pepper powder, ginger, scallions, crushed garlic, finely chopped mustard tuber and minced meat. Keep stir-frying until the oil turns red. Add the cooking wine, soy sauce, MSG, sugar, fish and some water. When it reaches a boiling point, turn to low fire until the dish is done. Then turn the fire to hot to thicken the sauce. It is now ready to serve.

Features：Dark red and brightly shiny.
Taste：Aromatically spicy.

干烧鱼
Dry-fried Fish

炒虾丁

主料：虾仁 350 克。

辅料：笋 50 克，青豌豆 50 克。

调料：料酒 5 克、味精 1 克、麻油 5 克、湿淀粉 25 克、油 60 克、盐 3 克、淀粉 10 克、鸡蛋清 1 只、清汤 50 克。

制作：①将虾仁洗净，滤干水份，放盐 2 克、鸡蛋清、淀粉搅拌上浆备用。

②将笋用刀切成 0.5 厘米见方小丁，青豌豆洗净备用。

③旺火烧锅，放油，待油温升至五成热时，倒入上好浆的虾仁，溜炒至断生，捞出。

④把原锅余油烧热，倒入笋丁，豌豆翻炒熟后，放清汤、盐 1 克、味精、料酒，调好口味，放湿淀粉勾芡，倒入虾仁，迅速翻炒，淋麻油出锅装盘。

特点：色泽斑斓

口味：鲜嫩爽滑

Stir-fried Shrimps with Bamboo and Peas

Ingredients:

350 grams (0.77lb) shrimps
50 grams (0.11lb) bamboo shoots
50 grams (0.11lb) green peas
5 grams (1tsp) cooking wine
1 gram (1/4tsp) MSG
5 grams (1tsp) sesame oil
25 gram (1.5tbsp) mixture of cornstarch and water
60 grams (4.5tbsp) cooking oil
3 grams (1/2tsp) salt
10 grams (1.5tbsp) dry cornstarch
1 egg white
50 grams (3tbsp) water

Directions:

(1) Wash the shrimps clean, drain off the water, add 2 grams (1/3tsp) of salt, egg white and dry cornstarch and mix.

(2) Cut bamboo shoots into dices of 0.5 cm (0.2in) each side. Wash the green peas clean and set aside.

(3) Heat the oil with a hot fire until 110-135℃ (230-275℉). Put in the marinated shrimps, quick-fry and remove from the wok.

(4) Heat the oil in the wok again. Put in the diced bamboo and green peas and stir-fry. Add water, 1 gram (1/6tsp) of salt, MSG and cooking wine. Put in the cornstarch-water mixture to thicken the sauce. Put in the shrimps and quickly stir-fry. Sprinkle the sesame oil and put on a serving dish.

Features: Very colorful.
Taste: Refreshing and succulent.

家常鱼

主料：鳜鱼1条（750克）

辅料：肉片、笋片、香菇片各25克。

调料：糖5克，盐2克，酱油30克，红辣椒3只，湿淀粉25克，葱段、姜末各5克，味精2克、油500克（实耗50克）料酒5克，清汤200克。

制作：①鱼宰杀后去鳃、内脏、鳞洗干净，在鱼身肉厚处剖一刀，用酱油抹遍鱼身备用。

②旺火烧锅放油，待油温升至七成热时改中火，放入鱼煎两面至七成熟时倒出滤油。

③原锅留余油20克，放入葱、姜煸出香味后，下红辣椒、肉片、笋片、香菇片，翻炒约1分钟后，放入鱼、料酒、酱油、盐、糖、味精、清汤烧沸后转小火烧15分钟，再转大火收浓卤汁勾芡，淋油即可出锅装盘。

特点：色泽金黄，汁浓味醇

口味：鱼肉鲜嫩，咸中略带甜

Home-style Fish

Ingredients:

1 freshwater manderin fish about 750 grams (1.65lb)
25 grams (0.9oz) sliced meat
25 grams (0.9oz) sliced bamboo shoots
25 grams (0.9oz) mushroom slices
5 grams (1tsp) sugar
2 grams (1/3tsp) salt
30 grams (1.6tbsp) soy sauce
3 hot chillies
25 grams (1.5tbsp) mixture of cornstarch and water
5 grams (0.18oz) sectioned scallions
5 grams (0.18oz) finely chopped ginger
2 grams (1/2tsp) MSG
500 grams (2 cups) cooking oil (only 50 grams or 4tbsp to be actually consumed)
5 grams (1tsp) cooking wine
200 grams (4/5 cup) water

Directions:

(1) Gut the fish, remove gills and scales. Make one cut where the meat is thick. Rub the fish with soy sauce.

(2) Heat oil over a hot fire and turn down to medium fire when the oil is 180-200℃ (355-390℉) hot. Deep-fry both sides of the fish until it is 70 percent done.

(3) Keep 20 grams (1.5tbsp) of oil in the wok. Put in the scallions and ginger until they give out an aroma. Put in the chilli, meat slices, bamboo shoots and mushrooms. Stir-fry for 1 minute and add the fish, cooking wine, soy sauce, salt, sugar, MSG and water. When mixture starts to boil, turn the fire to low and cook for 15 minutes. Turn the fire hot again to thicken the sauce. Sprinkle sesame oil and it is ready to serve.

Features: Golden in color with savory and rich sauce.
Taste: The fish is tender and the sauce has a slightly sweet taste.

家常鱼
Home-style Fish

脆皮虾

主料：虾 400 克。

辅料：面粉 250 克，淀粉 50 克。

调料：盐 3 克、味精 1 克、发酵粉 1-2 克、油 500 克（实耗 100 克）、料酒 10 克。

制作：①虾去掉头和身上的壳，留虾尾壳，洗净滤干水份，放盐 2 克，味精、料酒腌 15 分钟备用。

②面粉和淀粉加入水 250 克、盐 1 克、发酵粉、油 5 克，拌匀后，向一个方向搅拌成脆皮糊（脆皮糊是在面粉中放入淀粉、油和发酵粉搅成糊，附着在原料上经油炸后，外皮脆酥）备用。

③旺火烧锅放油，待油温升至三四成热时，用筷子夹住腌好的虾的尾巴，把虾在脆皮糊里蘸一下，挂糊（注意，虾尾不要挂上糊）后投入油锅中炸金黄色至熟，倒出滤油，装盘即可。上桌可蘸蕃茄或椒盐食用。

特点：色泽金黄

口味：外脆酥里嫩，香味独特

Crispy Shrimps

Ingredients：
400 grams (0.88lb) shrimp
250 grams (0.55lb) wheat flour
50 grams (8tbsp) dry cornstarch
3 grams (1/2tsp) salt
1 gram (1/4tsp) MSG
1-2 grams (1/4-1/2tsp) baking powder
500 grams (2 cup) cooking oil (only 100 grams or 8tbsp to be actually consumed)
10 grams (2tsp) cooking wine

Directions：
(1) Remove the heads and shells on the body of the shrimps, but keep the tail shells. Wash clean and drain off the water. Marinate with 2 grams (1/3tsp) of salt, MSG and cooking wine for 15 minutes.

(2) Add 250 grams (1 cup) of water, 1 gram (1/6tsp) of salt, the baking powder and 5 grams (1tsp) of oil to the dry cornstarch and flour and mix well into paste by stirring in one direction.

(3) Heat the oil over a hot fire until temperature reaches 50-100°C (120-210°F). Use chopsticks to hold the tail of the marinated shrimps and quickly dip each into the paste and then deep-fry until they are golden yellow. The shrimps can be served with tomato sauce or pepper salt. Make sure not to dip the tail in the paste.

Features: Beautiful golden color.

Taste: Crispy outside and tender inside with a unique delicious taste.

脆皮虾
Crispy Shrimps

脆皮鱼

主料：草鱼鱼肉 250 克。

辅料：面粉 250、淀粉 50 克。

调料：盐 3 克、味精 1 克、油 250 克（实耗 100 克）、料酒 10 克、发酵粉 2 克。

制作：①取去骨、刺、皮的净鱼肉切成 1 厘米宽的条，放盐 1 克，味精、料酒腌渍 15 分钟。

②面粉和淀粉加清水 250 克，盐 1 克、发酵粉、油 5 克，拌匀后，向一个方向搅拌成脆皮糊（见脆皮虾制作②）

备用。

③旺火烧锅放油，待油温升至三四成热时，用筷子夹住腌好的鱼条，在脆皮糊里蘸一下，挂糊，后投入油锅中炸成金黄色至熟，倒出滤油装盘即可。上桌可蘸茄酱或椒盐食用。

特点：色泽金黄

口味：外脆酥里嫩，香味独特

Crispy Fish

Ingredients：

250 grams (0.55lb) freshwater fish (grass carp) fillets

250 grams (0.55lb) wheat flour

50 grams (8tbsp) dry cornstarch

3 grams (1/2tsp) salt

1 gram (1/4tsp) MSG

250 grams (1 cup) cooking oil (100 grams or 8tbsp to be actually consumed)

10 grams (2tsp) cooking wine

2 grams (1/2tsp) baking powder

Directions：

(1) Cut the boneless and skinless fish fillets into thin slices of 1 cm (0.4in) in width. Add 1 gram (1/6tsp) of salt, MSG, and cooking wine and let marinate for 15 minutes.

(2) Add 250 grams (1 cup) of water, 1 gram (1/6tsp) of salt, the baking powder, 5 grams (1tsp) of oil to the flour and cornstarch and mix into paste by stirring in one direction.

(3) Heat the oil over a hot fire until it is about 50-100℃ (120-210℉). Use chopsticks to hold the fish slices, dip in the paste and deep-fry until golden yellow. They can be served with tomato sauce or pepper salt.

Features：Beautiful golden color.

Taste：Crispy outside and tender inside with a unique delicious taste.

脆皮鱼
Crispy Fish

铁排鱼

主料：鲳鱼 1 条约 500 克。

辅料：红辣椒丝 25 克。

调料：湿淀粉 25 克、番茄酱 100 克、辣酱油 25 克、糖 50 克、盐 2 克、味精 1 克、料酒 20 克、姜葱丝各 5 克、香醋 30 克、油 100 克（实耗 50 克）、清汤 100 克。

制作：①将鱼宰杀后去鳞、鳃、内脏，冲洗干净，用刀斜切成 1.5 厘米厚的块，用料酒腌渍 15 分钟。

②旺火烧锅，放油，待油温升至八成热时，放入鱼块逐块炸至金黄色后，倒出滤油。

③原锅留余油 10 克，放姜、葱、红辣椒丝，以及番茄酱、辣酱油、糖、盐、味精、清汤烧沸后调好口味，放香醋，湿淀粉勾芡后，倒入炸好的鱼块，翻烧均匀，淋油出锅，整齐排放在鱼盘中即成。

特点：色泽红润

口味：鱼肉鲜嫩

Stewed Fish Sections

Ingredients：

1 seawater butterfish of about 500 grams (1.1lb)
25 grams (0.9oz) red chillies (shredded)
25 grams (1.5tbsp) mixture of cornstarch and water
100 grams (5.5tbsp) ketchup
25 grams (2tbsp) chilli oil
50 grams (3.8tbsp) sugar
2 grams (1/3tsp) salt
1 gram (1/4tsp) MSG
20 grams (4tsp) cooking wine
5 grams (0.18oz) scallion shreds
5 grams (0.18oz) ginger shreds
30 grams (2tbsp) vinegar
100 grams (8tbsp) cooking oil (only 50 grams or 4tbsp to be actually consumed)
100 grams (6tbsp) water

Directions：

(1) Gut the fish, remove the scales and gills and wash the fish. Cut the fish sideways into chunks of 1.5 cm (0.6in) thickness and marinate in cooking wine for 15 minutes.

(2) Heat the oil in the wok until it is 200-220℃ (390-430℉). Deep-fry the fish chunks until they are golden brown. Remove them from the wok and drain off the oil.

(3) Keep 10 grams (2tsp) of oil in the wok. Put in ginger, scallions and chilli shreds. Add in the ketchup, hot chilli oil, sugar, salt, MSG and water and let ingredients boil. Add the vinegar and thicken the broth with the mixture of cornstarch and water. Put in the deep-fried fish chunks. Stir for even cooking. Sprinkle sesame oil and put the fish on a plate to serve.

Features：Beautiful with red color.
Taste：The fish is tender.

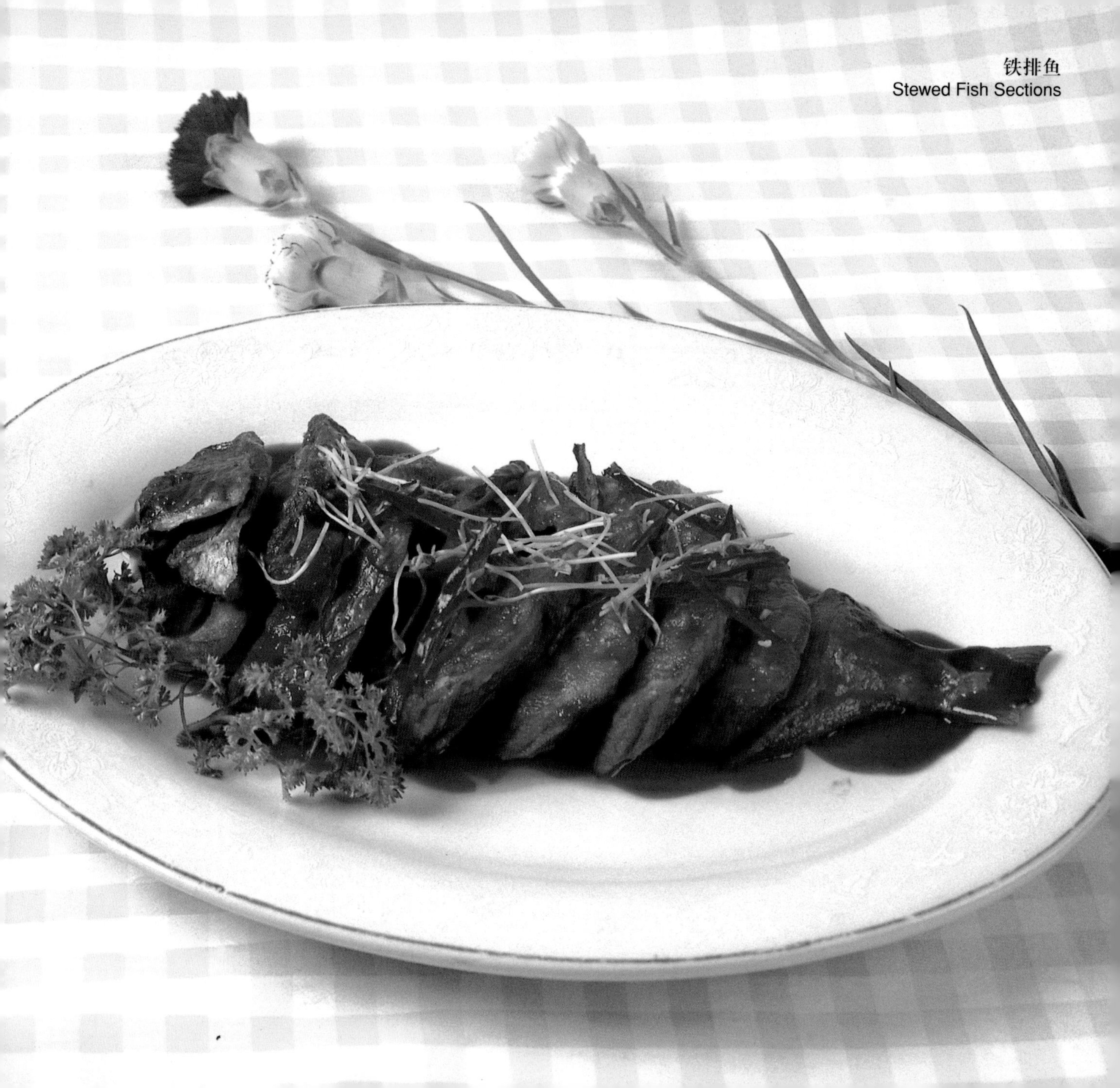

铁排鱼
Stewed Fish Sections

鱼肉双米

主料：草鱼鱼肉300克，鲜嫩玉米粒一罐约200克。

调料：盐4克、味精1克、清汤100克、鸡蛋清1只、淀粉5克、油50克、湿淀粉20克、料酒10克。

制作：①将除去骨、刺、皮的鱼肉切成0.5厘米见方的粒，放盐2克，鸡蛋清，淀粉，上浆备用。

②旺火烧锅，放油30克。待油温升至五成热时，放入鱼粒，滑炒开，至熟倒出。

③原锅烧热放油20克，放玉米、清汤、盐、味精、料酒，烧沸后调好口味，放湿淀粉勾芡，倒入鱼米翻炒均匀，淋油出锅即可。

特点：黄白相间

口味：鱼肉鲜嫩，咸鲜适口

Fish Cubes with Corn

Ingredients：
300 grams (0.66lb) freshwater fish (grass carp) meat
200 grams (0.44lb) canned fresh corn
4 grams (2/3tsp) salt
1 gram (1/4tsp) MSG
100 grams (6tbsp) water
1 egg white
5 grams (1tbsp) dry cornstarch
50 grams (4tbsp) cooking oil
20 grams (1tbsp) mixture of cornstarch and water
10 grams (2tsp) cooking wine

Directions：
(1) Cut the boneless and skinless fish into small square cubes of about 0.5 cm (0.2in) on each side. Add 2 grams (1/3tsp) of salt, the egg white, and cornstarch and let marinate.

(2) Heat 30 grams (2tbsp) of cooking oil until it is about 110-135℃ (230-275℉). Put in the fish cubes and stir-fry, then remove from the wok.

(3) Put the remaining 20 grams (1.5tbsp) of cooking oil in the wok and heat it. Put in the corn, water, salt, MSG, and cooking wine and let it boil. Add the mixture of cornstarch and water to thicken the sauce. Put in the fish cubes and stir. Sprinkle sesame oil and put on a plate to serve.

Features：Both yellow and white in color.
Taste：The fish is tender and fresh.

鱼肉双米
Fish Cubes with Corn

葡萄明虾

主料：虾 12 只。

辅料：面包一只。

调料：盐 3 克，味精 0.5 克，鸡蛋 2 只，淀粉 15 克，油 500 克（实耗 100 克）竹扦 12 根，料酒 15 克。

制作：①虾去头壳，留尾，放盐、味精、料酒、腌渍 10 分钟备用。

②面包揉碎。将腌过的明虾用竹杆从尾部插入虾身，拍上淀粉。

③鸡蛋打散，将拍上淀粉的虾，在鸡蛋中蘸一下，再在面包粒上滚一下，让它粘满面包粒，备用。

④旺火烧锅，放油，待油温升至六成热时，放入虾炸至熟，倒出滤油，装盘即成。

特点：色泽金黄，造型美观

口味：外脆里嫩、味鲜美

Deep-fried Crispy Prawns

Ingredients：
12 prawns bread crumbs
3 grams（1/2tsp）salt
0.5 gram（1/8tsp）MSG
2 eggs
15 grams（2.5tbsp）dry cornstarch
500 grams（2 cups）cooking oil（only 100 grams or 8tbsp to be actually consumed）
12 bamboo tooth picks
15 grams（1tbsp）cooking wine

Directions：
(1) Remove the prawn shells and tails and marinate for 10 minutes in salt, MSG and cooking wine.

(2) Put the tooth picks into the prawns to form their tails. Dust with cornstarch.

(3) Whip the eggs and dip the prawns in the whipped egg. Roll them in the bread crumbs.

(4) Heat the oil until it is about 135-170℃（275-340℉）and deep-fry the prawns fully covered with bread crumbs. Drain off the oil and put on a plate to serve.

Features：Golden brown in color and beautiful in appearance.
Taste：The prawns are crispy outside and tender inside.

葡萄明虾
Deep-fried Crispy Prawns

炒鲜贝

主料：鲜贝 300 克。

辅料：胡萝卜 25 克，青椒丁 25 克（丁为 1 厘米见方）。

调料：盐 3 克、味精 1 克、湿淀粉 20 克、清汤 50 克，以及葱姜各 2 克、熟猪油 50 克、料酒 5 克。

制作：①锅内放清水 1000 克烧沸，投入鲜贝"焯水"后，倒出滤干，放碗内，加盐 2 克，料酒 5 克，湿淀粉 10 克，上浆备用。

②旺火烧锅，放猪油 45 克，待油温升至四成热时，将鲜贝、胡萝卜丁、青椒丁入油锅滑炒至鲜贝呈白玉色倒出，装盘待用。

③原锅放熟猪油 5 克，放入葱姜煸出香味，加清汤、盐、味精，调好口味，勾芡，把鲜贝、胡萝卜丁、青椒丁倒入，翻炒后，淋油起锅，装盘（此菜要现做现吃，不然要出水）。

特点：白、红、绿相间，色泽悦目

口味：肉质鲜嫩

Stir-fried Fresh Scallops

Ingredients：
300 grams (0.66lb) fresh scallops
25 grams (0.9oz) carrot (diced to 1 cm or 0.39 in each side)
25 grams (0.9oz) green pepper (diced to 1 cm or 0.39 in each side)
3 grams (1/2tsp) salt
1 gram (1/4tsp) MSG
20 grams (1tbsp) mixture of cornstarch and water
50 grams (3tbsp) water
2 grams (0.07oz) scallions
2 grams (0.07oz) ginger
50 grams (0.11lb) cooked lard
5 grams (1tsp) cooking wine

Directions：
(1) Put 1,000 grams (4 cups) of water in the pot and bring it to boiling point. Quickly boil the fresh scallops and then drain off the water. Put the scallops in a bowl. Add 2 grams (1/3tsp) of salt, 5 grams (1tsp) of cooking wine, and 10 grams (1.5tsp) of cornstarch-water mixture and let marinate.

(2) Heat the wok over a hot fire, put in the 45 grams (0.1lb) of cooked lard and when the temperature is 70-135℃ (160-275℉), throw in the scallops, diced carrots and green peppers. Stir-fry still the scallops until they show a white crystal color. Put them on a plate.

(3) Put the remaining 5 grams (0.01lb) of cooked lard into the wok. Add the scallions and ginger until they produce their aroma. Add the water, salt, MSG, the cornstarch-water mixture, scallops, diced carrots and green peppers. Stir-fry and then put on a plate to serve. (This dish must be served immediately after cooking to prevent it from turning watery.)

Features: A welcome combination of white, red and green colors.

Taste: The scallops are very tender and juicy.

炒鲜贝
Stir-fried Fresh Scallops

计量换算表

1 磅	1 盎司	1 打兰	1 格令
约 454 克	约 28 克	约 1.8 克	约 0.06 克

调料 ml 勺	水	油	酱油	醋	料酒	盐	味精	砂糖	淀粉
1ml 勺	约 1 克	约 0.9 克	约 1.2 克	约 1 克	约 1 克	约 1.2 克	约 0.7 克	约 0.9 克	约 0.4 克
5ml 勺	约 5 克	约 4.5 克	约 6 克	约 5 克	约 5 克	约 6.3 克	约 3.7 克	约 4.5 克	约 2 克
15ml 勺	约 15 克	约 13.5 克	约 18 克	约 15 克	约 15 克	约 18.5 克	约 11 克	约 13 克	约 6 克
50ml 勺	约 50 克	约 55 克	约 60 克	约 50 克	约 50 克	约 63 克		约 42 克	约 20 克
500ml 勺	约 500 克	约 549 克	约 600 克	约 500 克	约 500 克	约 630 克			

A comparison of the weight systems

US system	1 grain(gr)	1ounce(oz)	1pound(lb)
Metric	0.065 gram(g)	28.35 grams(g)	454 grams(g)

A conversion table for measuring Chinese cooking ingredients*

ingredients cornstarch	water	ckg oil	soy sauce	vinegar	ckg wine	salt	MSG	sugar	cornstarch
1 pinch/1ml	1g	0.9g	1.2g	1g	1g	1.2g	0.7g	0.9g	0.4g
1tsp/5ml	5g	4.5g	6g	5g	5g	6.3g	3.7g	4.5g	2g
1tbsp/15ml	15g	13.5g	18g	15g	15g	18.5g	11g	13g	6g
1.76floz/50ml	50g	55g	60g	50g	50g	63g		42g	20g
3.52floz/1cup	500g	549g	600g	500g	500g	630g			

*All figures in grams given here are approximate as the exact equivalents will result
in too many digits after the decimal point.

在编辑《学做中国菜》系列丛书的过程中，得到了苏州饭店的大力支持和帮助。作为苏州市旅游业的骨干企业苏州饭店已有数十年的历史，饭店拥有一流的烹饪厨师，经验丰富，技艺精湛。今借此书出版之机，我们对苏州饭店给予的支持，深表感谢！

We wish to thank the Suzhou Hotel, which kindly provided strong support and assistance to the compilation of the *Learn to Cook Chinese Dishes* series. As a major tourist hotel in the city of Suzhou, the Suzhou Hotel has a history of dozens of years and is serviced by experienced first-class chefs.

图书在版编目(CIP)数据

学做中国菜·水产类/《学做中国菜》编委会编. – 北京:外文出版社,1999
ISBN 7-119-01130-8

Ⅰ.学… Ⅱ.学… Ⅲ.水产品-烹饪 Ⅳ.TS972.1
中国版本图书馆 CIP 数据核字(1999)第 45976 号

Members of the Editorial Board:
　　Sun Jiaping　Lu Qinpu
　　Sun Shuming　Liu Chun'gen
　　Lan Peijin
Dish preparation and text:
　　Zhu Deming　Wen Jinshu
　　Zhu Guifu　Zhang Guomin
　　Zhang GuoXiang　Xu Rongming
　　Cao Gang
Editor: Liu Chun'gen
English translating and editing:
　　Huang Youyi　Foster Stockwell　Cong Guoling
Design: Liu Chun'gen
Photography: Sun Shuming　Liu Chun'gen　Lan Peijin
Cover design: Wang Zhi

编委: 孙建平　鲁钦甫　孙树明
　　　　刘春根　兰佩瑾
菜肴制作及撰文: 朱德明　温金树
　　　　　　　　朱桂福　张国民
　　　　　　　　张国祥　徐荣明
　　　　　　　　曹　刚
责任编辑: 刘春根
英文翻译: 黄友义　卓柯达　丛国玲
设计: 刘春根
摄影: 孙树明　刘春根　兰佩瑾
封面设计: 王　志

First Edition 1999

Learn to Cook Chinese Dishes
——Seafood

ISBN 7-119-01130-8

©Foreign Languages Press
Published by Foreign Languages Press
24 Baiwanzhuang Road, Beijing 100037, China
Home Page: http://www.flp.com.cn
E-mail Addresses: info @ flp.con.cn
　　　　　　　　 sales @ flp.con.cn
Printed in the People's Republic of China

学做中国菜·水产类

《学做中国菜》编委会　编

ⓒ　外文出版社
外文出版社出版
(中国北京百万庄大街 24 号)邮政编码 100037
外文出版社网页:http://www.flp.com.cn
外文出版社电子邮件地址:info @ flp.con.cn
　　　　　　　　　　　　 sales @ flp.con.cn
北京骏马行图文中心制版
天时印刷(深圳)有限公司印制
1999 年 (24 开)第一版
1999 年第一版第一次印刷
(英汉)
ISBN 7-119-01130-8/J·1509 (外)
08000 (精)